Karel Čapek

COLUMBIA SLAVIC STUDIES

A Series of the Departmeut of Slavic Languages Columbia University

Karel Čapek

BY WILLIAM E. *edward* HARKINS

Columbia University Press

NEW YORK AND LONDON 1962

Library of Congress Catalog Card Number: 62-10148

Printed in The Netherlands

Preface

Karel Čapek is remembered today by most readers as a writer of utopian novels and plays; the current vogue of science fiction has revived interest in his work, and a number of new editions of his books have recently appeared in English. The enthusiasm for science fiction has also reached across the Iron Curtain to Czechoslovakia, Čapek's homeland, and to the Soviet Union and the other people's democracies, and in these lands Čapek's work has even been influential in helping to inspire younger writers in the genre. He is popular there also because his work brings welcome relief from the customary literary diet of socialist realism.

Čapek's novels and plays on scientific subjects were indeed significant, and sounded a prophetic warning on the dangers of modern warfare, technological civilization, and totalitarianism. Čapek even foresaw the possibility of using nuclear fission as a source of explosive energy for an atomic bomb. But it is not this part of his work which is most important. Rather his chief accomplishment lies in his effort to give a philosophical definition to the individual and his relation to a democratic society. Čapek's masterpiece is his trilogy of novels, *Hordubal, Meteor,* and *An Ordinary Life,* a work which René Wellek called collectively "one of the most successful attempts at a philosophical novel in any language." The trilogy is significant as great embodiment of the spirit of democratic humanism, and as such is almost without parallel in modern fiction.

In spite of Čapek's significance, no published study of book length on his life or his work exists in English, or indeed in any language save Dutch and Ukrainian. That there should be none in his own tongue—Czech— is the sad responsibility of history. Čapek's death occurred just before the Nazi occupation of Bohemia and Moravia in February, 1939. Under the occupation the publication of such a work remained impossible until the end of the war in 1945. And in February, 1948, the Communist coup brought an even tighter ban of silence concerning Čapek, who, as a "bourgeois" writer and the friend of T. G. Masaryk, was regarded as ideologically harmful to the new regime. This ban was later lifted in Čapek's homeland (though only after it had first been raised in the Soviet Union), and at the present writing it seems that two monographs, a biography and a critical study, will soon appear in Czechoslovakia.

The present book attempts to present a systematic account of Čapek's work for the Anglo-Saxon world, where he has always enjoyed an especial popularity, and to which he himself owed no small debt for literary and philosophical influence. The present study is primarily critical, but the first chapter presents a short biography; it should be pointed out that no definitive account of Čapek's life exists, and the chapter in question, for all its shortcomings, gives perhaps the most comprehensive and balanced treatment of any published work now in existence. In the critical part of the study, I am concerned first of all with philosophical ideas, second with artistic structure, devices, and innovations in form; I have also striven to keep in view the relation of these two aspects to one another. It was my original intention to deal with the whole of Čapek's work, including the voluminous essays, sketches, feuilletons, and tales for children. But an adequate treatment of these lesser genres would have rendered the study extremely diffuse, and would have necessitated a good deal of rather tedious description, as well as elaboration of the obvious. The charm of these lesser forms is perhaps too intangible and intimate to be captured readily in criticism; the reader can only be advised to read these works for himself, and in particular the hilarious *Gardener's Year* and the volume of essays called in English *Intimate Things*. The present study concerns only Čapek's fiction and his plays.

Titles of Čapek's writings are given throughout in English, but an appendix supplies the original Czech titles. Titles and dates of published English translations are given in the appropriate footnote.

A brief word about pronunciation. Czech vowels are pronounced approximately like the corresponding vowels in Spanish. The signs ʹ and ° over a vowel indicates length. The sign ˇ over the consonants *c* and *s* indicates equivalents of the English *ch* and *sh* respectively. The Czech digraph *ch* has the same pronunciation as in German.

I wish to acknowledge my sincere gratitude to a host of people who have generously given help and advice. First of all I am indebted to Olga Scheinpflugová, Čapek's widow, and to Jarmila Čapková, the widow of Josef Čapek, for graciously permitting me twice to visit the Čapek residence in Vinohrady. Dr. Miroslav Halík, Čapek's editor and the faithful guardian of his heritage, has been of inestimable assistance in helping to obtain materials difficult of access. Professor Otakar Vočadlo, Čapek's good friend, also deserves my warmest thanks for his suggestions, as does Professor Otakar Odložilík. Mrs. Božena Albrecht has generously lent me many items from her fine collection of materials on Čapek. Jindřich Chalupecký and Robert Davison have willingly volunteered help in specific research tasks. Professor Albert Hofstadter and Professor George Kline deserve thanks for advice on specific problems of philosophical history. I am indebted to Mr. Howard Israel and Mr. Sanford Kadet for invaluable suggestions on literary questions. Mr. Richard Astor and Professor Edgar Lehrman have generously contributed advice on matters of style, as has my editor, Miss Joan McQuary, to whom I am greatly indebted. Mrs. Božena Bradbrook and Mr. Deryck Viney have kindly permitted me to quote from their unpublished studies on Karel Čapek and Josef Čapek, respectively. I am also much indebted to the staff of the Reference Room of the Columbia University Library. I wish to thank the John Simon Guggenheim Memorial Foundation and the Inter-University Committee for Travel Grants for their financial assistance, which has made this study possible. Finally, acknowledgment is due to the editors of *PMLA* and *The Slavic and East European Journal* for permission to quote certain passages from articles written by me on specific aspects of Čapek's work.

Columbia University W. E. H.
November, 1961

Contents

1. An Ordinary Life?

The village of Malé Svatoňovice in northwestern Bohemia, the birth-place of Karel Čapek, lies at the western end of the Krkonoše (Giant) Mountains, in a land of magnificent scenery—and of coal mines and heavy industry. The town was close to the Austro-German (later the Czechoslovak-German) border, as well as to the linguistic frontier between Czech- and German-speaking peoples; the Munich accord of 1938 was to award this area to Hitler's Germany.

When Karel Čapek was born here, on January 9, 1890, it was a region rich in tradition; here Božena Němcová and Alois Jirásek, two great Czech romantic writers, had been born and grew up. The natives still told enthralling stories of Krakonoš, the legendary giant of these mountains.

Karel remembered his mother, Božena Čapková, with special tenderness, though her hysterical anxiety and hypochondria must have disturbed him as a child. She was a high-strung, sensitive intellectual who suffered from nervousness and ill health. She took drugs to quiet her nerves, and her premature death was perhaps due to an overdose of these. As a young girl she had been very pretty, but her childhood was unhappy, marred by the brutality of her father. She had a large library and subscribed to a number of cultural and literary reviews. Her reading preferences were the Czech symbolist Antonín Sova, Zola, and Josef Šlejhar, a Czech naturalist. To the children she read from K. J. Erben's romantic ballads, declaiming them with pathos and dramatic intonations. An amateur ethnographer, she recorded folk songs, tales, and popular sayings. The old peasant story tellers who crowded into the family kitchen were a source of great interest to Karel as well as to his elder brother, Josef, though their mother did not always permit the children to stay and listen. Both brothers were to retain a lively interest in folk art; Karel, who read little fiction in later life, once confessed that he preferred fairy tales above all other reading.[1] His later love for colloquial speech and popular expressions may also stem from this influence.

Something of his mother's constant anxiety was communicated to Karel, who avoided high-strung people in later life, fearing that he too might become a victim of nerves. His wife, Olga Scheinpflugová, wrote of him later that the suffered from a phobia about health and from depression, a kind of "neurasthenia," as she put it.[2] Čapek himself recalled how his mother would pray for his health at the local shrine of the Virgin, which had some reputation for its miraculous cures. There she would bring wax models of the human chest as an offering to induce the strengthening of the boy's delicate lungs.[3]

The practice and avocations of his father, Antonín Čapek, a country doctor, kept him too busy for much companionship with the children. The brothers recall the skeleton which stood in his reception room, an eloquent symbol of death, as well as the scenes of suffering which they saw there. The poor miners who came for treatment but who could not pay were probably the boys' chief contact with poverty and with the industrial life of the region. Dr. Čapek was a typical provincial intellectual: he made public speeches, was president of an amateur theatrical troupe, collected funds for the local museum, wrote verses, and painted. Gardening was a favorite avocation for him, as it was to be later for both Karel and Josef. Despite the apparent community of his interests with those of his wife, there seems to have been a lack of sympathy between them, and with her neurotic sensitivity she found him crude and rough. A rationalist by temperament, he was a confirmed atheist.

The most interesting personality in the family was the maternal grandmother. Josef Čapek believes that her fluent folk speech, rich in proverbs, bywords, and rhymed phrases, helped form the "rich, pithy, flexible and, at the same time, simple language of Karel

Čapek." He pays tribute to her courage, her common sense, and to her responsiveness to the range of experience in her limited world.[4] In his collection *The Limping Pilgrim* (1936), Josef quotes a sample of her rhymed peasant wit: "Zadnice a čelo, to je jedno tělo" (The backside and the forehead—it's all the same body). A miller's daughter and the wife of a miller, she suffered stoically the tyrannical temper of her drunkard husband, a handsome lecher who betrayed her frequently and even dragged her about by her hair.

Curiously enough, no portrayal of his grandmother's strong personality appears in any of Karel's fictional works, though the character of Nána, the old nurse in *R.U.R.*, may bear a slight resemblance. In *An Ordinary Life* (1934), a novel full of childhood reminiscences, there are recognizable portraits of his father and mother, but the grandmother is missing, as are Karel's brother and sister. This last omission may be explained by their still being alive in 1934, while the parents were not.

There were three children in all in the family. Helena Čapková, the eldest, was born in 1886; later she became a minor writer whose best work was a volume of lyrical reminiscences of childhood: *A Little Girl* (1920). His sister Helena may have influenced the portrayal of certain of Karel's idealized heroines, and in *R.U.R.* Helena Glory actually bears her name.

Josef Čapek was born the next year, almost three years before Karel. The two brothers were to be very close throughout their lives. They began their literary career jointly as the Brothers Čapek, and collaborated again several times in later life. Josef became a talented painter and writer in his own right, as well as the illustrator of several of Karel's books. The sturdier Josef looked after the weaker Karel; "Watch out for Karel; Karel is tender, weak, and such gifted people sometimes die young," he remembers his mother saying, and she begged him to be a protector and guide to his younger brother.[5] In fact Karel, born prematurely, was always tender and inclined to be sickly, the favorite of his mother. His childhood was a sunny one, and apparently his mother's solicitude did not spoil him. Although the two older children were sensitive to Karel's sickliness, they did not permit him to be pampered; Josef introduced him to the joys of outdoor life and taught him to climb trees. Early the brothers developed their own private jargon, a sophisticated combination of deformed words, literary references, puns, and nonsense, and in adult life they often reverted to it. Karel was later to feel lonely and depressed when separated from Josef. From 1925 they shared the same house in Prague, and each was the other's closest friend, though their intimacy was partly interrupted by their subsequent marriages. In spite of the sincere affection he felt for Karel, Josef could not always understand his brother's greater popularity, and in a Nazi concentration camp he is reported to have said that most of his independent literary works were endowed with some measure of "protest" against Karel's writings.[6]

Karel Čapek later recalled that he had begun to write at the age of eight, when he composed some verses for his father's birthday.[7] In his second year at elementary school he began to do his homework in verse. At that time he thought of becoming a doctor, but in his thirteenth year he began to think seriously of a career as a writer.

In 1901, when he was about eleven, Karel was sent to high school in Hradec Králové in eastern Bohemia. At thirteen he first fell in love, and wrote verses to the girl, as well as deeply serious and adult letters in which, posing as a man of the world, he offered to show her wonders she as yet knew nothing of. His first published poems appeared in 1904 in a regional newspaper under the name of "Simple Themes"[8]; this title, and perhaps the sentimental flavor of the poems, was borrowed from the Czech nineteenth-century writer Jan Neruda, who later influenced Čapek's journalistic style so strongly. The first poem describes an autumn landscape, with a father carrying a coffin for his dead child. In the second, a hungry child asks where her father is; he is on his way home from a tavern, drunk. A month later a fairy tale ("Pohádka") appeared in the same paper. Čapek also contributed regularly to the school newspaper during his last years in high school.

In the autobiographical preface to *The Garden of Krakonoš*, the brothers write that Karel had to leave Hradec Králové because he was a member of an anarchist society. Such secret political societies, though not permitted by the authorities, were then common among the students of Austrian high schools. Presumably Karel was expelled from school when his membership was discovered.

From Hradec Králové Karel went on to high school in Brno, in
Moravia, where he lived with his sister Helena, who was now
married. He remained in Brno from 1905 to 1907, when he moved
to Prague with his family. His father had retired from practice, and
he and his wife now came to Prague to make a home for the two
sons. Čapek completed high school there, and, probably in 1909,
enrolled as a student in Charles University, with philosophy as his
major discipline. Meanwhile Josef, resisting the family's attempts to
make him the manager of a textile factory, had come there to study
painting. The two began their literary collaboration late in 1907.
Their first story, "The Return of the Prophet Hermotinos," was
published in the newspaper *Lidové noviny* on January 18, 1908.[9] It
was followed by an ever-increasing stream of stories, causeries,
articles, aphorisms, and reviews of books and paintings, published
in various Prague journals and papers.

Much has been speculated about the working methods of the
Brothers Čapek. They themselves preferred to maintain the pretense
that they always created jointly and together. Josef Čapek later
recalled that their collaboration had begun when Karel was dissatisfied with a story and threw it away. Josef saved and reworked
it; Karel then reworked it again, and they published it under the
signature of the "Brothers Čapek," which the public at first often
took for a pseudonym. The cosmopolitan tone of their stories even
led to a rumor that the real author was French. František Langer
supposes that they would plan their subjects together before they
wrote; then one would write, and the other would suggest revisions.
Ladislav Bulín, extrapolating from their later, independent writings,
supposes that Josef is the primary author of passages where there
are lyrical repetitions; Karel of those in which there are paradoxes
of disparate, illogically associated ideas. But these discriminations
are perhaps too neat.[10]

The two brothers made a dandified impression on the streets of
Prague, with their straw hats with broad bands, double-breasted
jackets, and American Walk-Over shoes. Broad-shouldered, each
walked with his head in the air, and Karel carried a cane.[11] They
frequented the Unionka, a Bohemian café, appearing regularly
twice a week in the afternoon; there they met young writers such as

František Langer, Petr Křička, and Eduard Bass. The two brothers
were inseparable, and frequently surprised others by communicating
to each other in their private jargon. Their literary sophistication
was in strange contrast to their lack of actual experience of the world,
and they seemed an odd blend of the witty sophisticate and the
provincial *ingénu*. Josef Čapek once remarked that at the time they
were much more interested in girls than in literary fame, and were
terrified lest the young ladies they met at dances might identify
them as the writers of the cynical, frequently erotic causeries.
Fortunately this never occurred.[12]

In summer, 1910, Josef Čapek removed to Paris to continue his
art studies, and in fall of that year Karel went to Berlin to attend
the university. Thus their collaboration was broken off. Although it
was resumed the following year for a brief time, most of their subsequent writing was independent.

In 1911 Karel went to France, spending the summer with Josef
in Marseilles and in Paris. A French painter named Chauliac introduced them to occasional glimpses of Paris cabarets. Čapek later
remarked that Paris had influenced him much more than Berlin, for
in the latter city he had only attended university, while in Paris he
saw night life as well.[13] In Paris Karel acquired his enthusiasm for
the philosophy of Bergson, who, along with the American pragmatists, became the principal influence on his thought. His strong
interest in avant-garde French literature and painting also began at
this time.

The brothers returned to Prague in autumn, 1911, and Karel
resumed his studies at Charles University. He took his doctor's
degree in 1915, writing his dissertation on "Objective Methods in
Esthetics."[14] A legacy of 2,000 crowns a year (about $ 500 in
American money of that time) helped the brothers eke out their
slim earnings from literature. Meanwhile Karel's literary work
continued, though he published less during these years. In 1916 the
brothers brought out their first book, *The Luminous Depths*, a
collection of tales most of which had originally appeared in various
journals in 1910–12.

Poor health exempted Čapek from military service during the
war years. Calcification had appeared in several vertebrae of his

spine, perhaps the result of an attack of scarlet fever as a child. It became difficult for him to turn his head, and he walked with a cane. The pain was at times intense, but his wife later said that he always rejected the sympathies of others and rarely complained. Once he met a medical student who astonished him with the information that his illness was very rare, and that at the Faculty of Medicine in Prague they called it "Čapek's disease."

Throughout the war Čapek remained a firm believer in the Allied cause, and once hinted jokingly that he had considered buying a revolver and assassinating an important Austrian personage.[15] Hoping to work for Czech independence abroad, he applied for permission to visit Spain to study the unique architectural style of the Pyrenees country. After a long police interview in which he was questioned about his stay in France, permission was refused. When America entered the war in 1917, he returned to work on his treatise on pragmatism (*Pragmatismus*, 1918) as a pro-American gesture.

Poor health prevented Čapek from taking work which might be too taxing; he also desired time for writing. Hence, in 1916, he accepted the post of tutor to the son of Count Vladimír Lažanský on the count's estate near Žlutice in western Bohemia. The old count addressed his tenants with the intimate singular. Though German was his mother tongue and he spoke Czech badly, he had no sympathy for Austria; he dreamt, rather, of the revival of an independent Bohemian kingdom. He allowed only Czech to be spoken at his château; the count alone was exempted from his own rule and permitted to employ German. During the war he never bothered to conceal his pro-Czech, anti-Austrian sympathies, and once was almost arrested in Prague for making a scene in a hotel. The orchestra was playing "Wacht am Rhein" for the Austrian officers there; in Czech Prague "Wacht am Rhein" might never be played, he vociferated. Čapek relates that on their first interview the count began in Czech but was evidently relieved when Čapek went over to German. "Sagen Sie, Herr Doktor, werden wir siegen oder die Anderen?" "Which side, Count? Do you mean Austria?" "Aber nein. Wir Russen. Wir Franzosen."[16]

Life on the estate assured Čapek of enough food during wartime.

But he remained there less than a year, from the end of 1916 through
the summer of 1917, when he left to begin a career as a journalist.
The Emperor Charles, on his coronation in May, 1917, had pro-
claimed an amnesty for political prisoners. Karel Kramář, leader of
the middle-of-the-road National Democrats, was released from
prison, and his paper *Národní listy* began to reappear. This gave
Čapek an opportunity for employment which had not existed during
the earlier years of the war. He went to work on Kramář's paper,
and the following year was made literary and art editor. *Wayside
Crosses*, a collection of metaphysical tales, appeared in 1917 as Karel's
first independent collection.

The year 1918 saw the publication of Karel's treatise on pragmatism, as well as a selection of the brothers' earlier sketches and
aphorisms from the period 1908–12, *The Garden of Krakonoš*. Karel
edited two collections of fairy tales, *Nůše pohádek* (1918–20), to
which he also contributed, as well as a dictionary of modern art,
Musaion (1920–21). Meanwhile, both brothers contributed to *Nebojsa*
(1918–20), a humorous and satirical magazine for which Karel (under
the pen-name of Plocek) wrote some amusing satirical verses on
current events. And in 1920 he published a volume of translations of
modern French poetry, from Baudelaire to Apollinaire, a work
which greatly influenced the development of Czech poetry. Čapek's
first play to reach the stage, *The Outlaw*, had its première at the
National Theater in Prague on March 2, 1920.

It was around 1920 that Čapek began his lifelong friendship with
the actress Olga Scheinpflugová. Their attachment would presumably have culminated in an immediate marriage, but poor health
forced Čapek to abandon this hope. Still the two remained friends,
and when much later, in 1935, a Viennese doctor told Čapek that his
spinal disease was now quiescent, they were finally married. Meanwhile Olga had become a leading stage star and popular writer;
when they first met in 1920, however, she was still a relatively unknown player at the Malé Theater in Prague. She was twelve years
his junior. Čapek, who knew her father, a fellow journalist, came
backstage to meet her. He had read a story of hers published in a
Sunday paper, and told her that it contained "much nonsense and
much talent." He asked her to read the part of the heroine in his

Outlaw, since she had a good voice for it. The role was already cast, so that Olga was only to understudy it—perhaps a pretext on Čapek's part to meet her. Only much later, when *The Outlaw* was revived, did she play the role of Mimi.

Čapek's next play, *R.U.R.*, which introduced the word robot to the world's languages, opened at the National Theater on January 25, 1921. Destined to be Čapek's greatest popular success, it was soon translated and played in almost all the civilized countries of the world and became one of the most widely performed plays of the century. Such a phenomenon was quite unparalleled in Czech literature, and Čapek was hailed as the outstanding Czech writer of his generation.

But envy was the natural result, and critics began to accuse him—quite irrationally and unjustifiably—of tailoring his work to suit international taste and neglecting the spiritual needs of his people. The younger generation of poets was quick to forget that Čapek himself had only recently been a leading member of the Czech avant-garde, and now attacked him for catering to popular taste. This accusation was largely unwarranted; *R.U.R.*, though conventional enough in some respects, was one of the first Czech expressionistic plays. Still, there is some truth in the charge, for as Čapek developed, his art became more conservative. The change was no doubt consequent on age and, perhaps, the effect of his journalistic work on his other writing. But, though he later lost much of the militant modernist spirit of his youth, he never faltered in a search for originality as well as expressive significance. In style, genre. and in the ability to embody philosophical ideas in literary form, his later writing, and particularly his work published between 1929 and 1936, is more strikingly original than the sometimes imitative avant-gardism of his youth.

The great success of *R.U.R.* was almost repeated in the next play, *From the Insect World* (1921), co-authored with Josef Čapek. It, too, was staged all over Europe and in America. An allegory in which insects symbolize human vices, it is perhaps the more theatrically effective of the two plays.

Emboldened by his success on the stage, Čapek accepted the post of director at the Prague City Theater, where *From the Insect World*

was premièred. He remained there from 1921 to 1923, staging
thirteen plays in all, as well as one at the National Theater. He
directed three plays by Molière (with Otokar Fischer he translated
Sganarelle into Czech in 1922), his own *Makropulos Secret* (1922),
and his brother's *Land of Many Names* (1923). His production of
Shelley's *The Cenci* in 1922 was very likely the first on the continent.

Critics and actors have praised his direction. Miroslav Rutte
writes that as a director he emphasized parody and comedy of body
movement, "a childlike delight in absurdity, in clownish exaggeration of movements and forms, of mechanical parody of man."[17] This
"Chaplin-like" trait of Čapek's work may be observed in his writing
as well; he too could capture the comedy and pathos of the figure of
the "little man." Indeed, his facial appearance as a young man and
awkward walk (with a cane) made him look a bit like Chaplin.

In spite of the relative success of these three plays (*The Makropulos Secret* was also translated and played abroad), Čapek seems to
have become increasingly disillusioned with the stage. *Adam the
Creator* (1927), written with Josef Čapek, had a lesser success. He
declared that he was dissatisfied with writing for the theater because
plays were only a "half creation," and too much depended on the
director and the actors.[18] For ten years following 1927 he wrote no
more plays. This fact alone suggests that he was not preoccupied
with considerations of success, for his plays won far more fame than
his novels, tales, or articles. And, indeed, success brought him surprisingly little money. German royalties were paid in inflated
currency, while none came from America, since Czechoslovakia did
not subscribe to the international copyright convention. An American
film company seeking to produce *R.U.R.* lost interest when it discovered that it could not obtain exclusive rights to the work. When
this fact became known in Czechoslovakia, indignant attacks on
America appeared in the papers. But Čapek pointed out that in fact
it was Czechoslovakia who was at fault, since she had never subscribed to the convention. He added that an American agent had
even advised him to publish first not in Czechoslovakia, but in
America, in order to secure an international copyright.[19]

In March, 1921, the brothers left *Národní listy* to go over to *Lidové
noviny*, a middle-of-the-road paper edited by their old friend Eduard

Bass. At the time many National Democrats had become dissatisfied with their party's opposition to Tomáš Masaryk, the first president of the young republic. They withdrew their support from
Národní listy and went over to *Lidové noviny*, which now became the
more important paper. Apparently the brothers accepted Bass's
offer because there was a danger that Josef might lose his position
on *Národní listy*, since that paper had too little work for him.[20]
Karel soon completed a first novel, *Factory for the Absolute* (1922),
which appeared in *Lidové noviny* in regular installments. He remained on the staff of *Lidové noviny* for the rest of his life, though he
often contributed to other journals. Curiously enough, though Čapek
deserted the theater both as author and director, he never gave up
journalism, in spite of the fact that it obligated him fill a column
regularly, even daily at some periods. Apparently he felt a constant
need to write, to express himself on every conceivable subject. The
newspaper column and feuilleton were forms which suited the wide
range of his interests: philosophical, esthetic, scientific, political,
and social, as well as literary. In this preference for a combination
of journalism and literature he much resembled Chesterton, whom
he greatly admired, though the range of his interests was broader
and his wit more humane.

To those who protested that newspaper work was beneath the
dignity of a world-famous author or that it might have a harmful
influence on his serious writing, Čapek was firm in defending his
right to practice journalism. It is not the writer who is out of place
in journalism, he insisted, but the many journalists who demean a
noble profession, when they might better be employed in a government or business office.[21] He seems to have felt deeply his responsibility as an enlightener and *Kulturträger*, not in a narrowly didactic,
but in a broader cultural and spiritual sense. Perhaps he betrayed an
unconscious vanity in this, but it must be said that the sum total of
his journalistic writing, with all its ups and downs, embodies the
spiritual testament of one of the most humane, civilized, and
flexible minds of our century.

Čapek's constant need to write was not satisfied by journalism
alone. Once he remarked that he wanted to produce at least a hundred
books and to attempt all literary genres.[22] Only his premature death

at forty-eight seems to have prevented him from fulfilling this
ambition. Though he was a fluent writer, the task of composition
was not entirely easy for him:

I work with relative difficulty and with effort; to be sure I write whatever the saliva brings to my tongue [a Czech saying], but I try as hard as
possible to say it clearly. When the thing is clearly expressed, it at once
becomes evident whether it is truthful or false, reasonable or stupid,
good or bad. I never enjoy writing, but feel enraged and stubborn, and
bite my penhandle. I cannot understand how one can dictate to a typist,
without trying to crush either her or the typewriter in his teeth.

My greatest weakness is a certain inability to concentrate. I can think
as little without a pen in hand as a tailor can sew without a needle; I plan
very little in advance, and my thought is simultaneously its own expression; if I cannot speak or write, I am as dumb as a stump and flighty as
a sparrow. Besides, I am unusually easy-going, and if I work all the time
and turn out much, then it is to avoid getting bored.[23]

Later Čapek added: "For the most part I write aloud. I must say
the sentence over to see how it sounds."[24] And Olga Scheinpflugová
observed that while Čapek worked on a novel or play, he read only
detective stories in English or French, and this deliberately so that
he would not be influenced by the style of the book he was reading.

Čapek writes further of his work:

I take no special pleasure in fiction or in the theater; I read very few
novels or stories and very much non-fiction; the theater I attend only by
sheer chance.[25] I think this is because I cannot abide sitting passively,
and I somehow resist letting myself be carried away by anyone else. The
best thing is to write something oneself; otherwise, I think, literature
would be unbearable for me...

To understand, that is my great and unquenchable passion; I suppose
that the reason I write is to understand. I should perhaps have made a
fairly good specialist... if I had been able to restrict myself to one field;
unfortunately I am interested in everything that exists, so I can do no
more than be a writer.

To understand is my one mania; to express is another. Not to express
myself, but to express things [a sentence which contains the key to
Čapek's esthetics]. I believe that I have succeeded in expressing many
things briefly and almost precisely. In my plays I have achieved a certain
success by trying to find a real colloquial speech, never a written language.
To provide reading matter is a writer's business; for that he is paid, as it

were. But to create living dialogue, to perfect the language, to give full value to human speech, this is a special national and social mission; in it one can reap a hidden and mysterious harvest.

Influences, influences—that question puzzles me. If I must admit to them, then it is a case of *embarras de richesses*. I think that the greatest literary influences on me were my childhood reading,[26] folk speech, and Latin prose; then everything else, good or bad, which I ever read. Perhaps I could mention three or four authors who have *not* influenced me; otherwise I seek to learn from everyone who comes to my hand; I set no great store on originality. In literature it is as in business life; the rich live openly on the work of other people. As for me, I belong rather to those who would contribute to a future store of riches, and I should be grateful to those who might come to use it. I do not do it for my own sake.[27]

Olga describes Čapek at this period as slender in body, with a long, fine face and a high forehead. His lips were "those of a Negro child." These, with his immense eyes, were his most striking feature. Photographs show a face which was boyish, lively, and flexible, and with a bit of the clown in it, not unlike Chaplin or Fernandel. Čapek smoked almost constantly, breaking the cigarettes in half and inserting them in a holder. His behavior was a wonderful mixture of the serious and the childlike. He was shy, nervous, afraid of crowds; rarely did he go to the theater, and his visits to the cinema were made only in the afternoon, when he could sit alone. His clothes were untidy and unpressed, and were covered with the ashes he absentmindedly strewed from his eternal cigarette. He loved witty conversation, and his speech was a flow of puns and jokes. Some of these were brilliant, but in the unchecked stream of wit Čapek was not always too discriminating.

It is true that Čapek's decision not to marry Olga was based on the advice of a physician, and the pain which he suffered from his spine and his headaches, along with his fear of nervous excitement, probably confirmed him in this resolution, but it must also be said that he showed himself temperamentally unsuited for marriage. His life was crowded with his work and his many interests, and these seem to have brought him his greatest happiness. In the early 1920s his works, such as *The Makropulos Secret* and *Krakatit*, are filled with a passionate eroticism which presumably reflects his intense disappointment at the frustration of his hopes. But by the end of the

1920s, erotic motifs almost disappear from his work. His novel *Hordubal* (1933), in which a gentle peasant voluntarily accepts sexual rejection by his wife, and even tolerates her infidelity, suggests that Čapek had resigned himself to a single life. When he finally married Olga in 1935, he insisted on moving to the third floor of his house, abandoning the first two floors to her; upstairs he could work alone, cosy and contented, especially when he heard the patter of rain on the roof.

This was the double house which the brothers had built in 1925 on Úzká Street (since renamed Street of the Brothers Čapek), in the upper-middle-class district of Vinhorady. Karel occupied one side, decorating it with paintings, especially those by Josef Čapek and other contemporary Czech painters. Josef, one of the leading Czech artists, had developed an original and striking primitive style, based in part on cubist and expressionist influences. A connoisseur of Persian carpets, Karel acquired a collection with which he covered the floors and some of the walls. The ample yard gave him an opportunity for the first of a long series of avocations—gardening. He worked at it intensively, growing rare plants, even Alpine flowers. Photographs of his flowers appeared in several magazines, and he contributed reviews on gardening books to the *Prager Presse*. Later he added a greenhouse for orchids and cacti. He and his brother, who shared his enthusiasm, worked in their old clothes, and Karel was never so pleased as when a deliveryman would approach and ask him rudely if Dr. Čapek were at home.

Another hobby, which developed late in the 1920s, was photography. Čapek's favorite subjects were flowers, dogs and cats (which he kept as pets), or simple objects, such as old shoes or a pair of scales. He used his photographs to illustrate one of his books: *Dashenka; or, the Life of a Puppy* (1932), and several others can be found in the posthumous collection of essays, *The Things around Us* (1954). The technical quality of his photographs is high; artistically their value is questionable, but the pictures of inanimate objects are surprisingly fresh in their simplicity and expressiveness. His choice of such subjects illustrates his philosophy of art: to express things and never himself. In fact, they are more consistent in this than are his novels or plays.

Another enthusiasm was nature study, and his special interests were for wild flowers, butterflies, and birds. Čapek also collected phonograph records, particularly folk music, from all parts of the world. His wife recalls that a recording of Cuban music inspired him while he was working on his novel, *Meteor* (1934), the scene of which is laid in the West Indies, and that the record played constantly while he was writing.

Čapek had remarkable powers of observation, and could lose himself completely in the contemplation of objects. Thus he could spend hours watching birds, or pass an entire trip by train in winter observing the formation of "ice flowers" on the car window.

Travel was another source of pleasure, though Čapek's trips were never long or extravagant. He visited Italy (1923), England (1924), Spain (1930), Holland (1932), and Scandinavia (1936), and made several excursions to Slovakia. In England he was welcomed by well-known literary personalities: Shaw, Wells, Galsworthy, Sir Nigel Playfair, and others. Of all the peoples he visited, he was closest, no doubt, to the English. Indeed, his Czech critics have often accused him of adopting the pose (or at least of attempting it) of an English gentleman. But in fact he was very far from being English in his attitudes toward life. Once he remarked to Olga that he considered the English politically backward, almost thirty years behind the Continent. On his return from England, he was interviewed by Dorothy Thompson and told her that England had terrified him, particularly London, with its masses of people. If there are so many people, he remarked, then human life cannot be worth much. The prospect of visiting America frightened him even more; he planned to make the trip, however, but never did.[28] The remarkable popularity of his writings, particularly of his plays, in England and America, was in part made possible by the influence on his work of English writers, of Wells, Chesterton, and Shaw. But their influence was hardly greater than that of the French: of Anatole France, the *unanimistes*, of Jules Lemaître and Pierre Mac Orlan, and of French cubist esthetics.

All of Čapek's interests are reflected in his literary work. Each of the travels to foreign countries resulted in a book of sketches. There are also collections on gardening, domestic animals, the seasons of the year, and the world of objects about us. Oriental carpets are the subject of two of the *Tales from the Other Pocket* (1929); another of these tales deals with the mania of a cactus enthusiast who steals rare specimens from a famous collection. Josef Čapek illustrated several of the collections of "hobby books" in his characteristic and witty style, but earlier Karel had already begun to produce his own simple line drawings as illustrations; these served in foreign countries, where Josef, now married, did not accompany him.

Čapek played an active part in the Prague P.E.N. Club, and was elected its president in 1925. He also inspired the formation of a P.E.N. Club in Slovakia. But public attacks eventually led him to resign his position. As president of the club, he appeared to be an official spokesman for Czech literature, which he did not wish; in a letter to Masaryk, who had opposed his resignation, he argued that he could be of more value to his country as an independent.

In 1935 H. G. Wells expressed a wish that Čapek should succeed him as president of the International P.E.N. Club, and Čapek finally agreed to accept. But lack of time and nervous strain made him unable to attend the world congress of the club in Buenos Aires that year, and as a result he was not elected.

In 1924 Čapek founded an informal society of writers, artists, politicians, and academicians, the so-called Pátečníci, or "Friday Circle," which met weekly at his home. Originally planned as an artistic discussion group, it broadened into a society with wider interests and a vaguely liberal political orientation. The members numbered about twenty-five, including Josef Čapek, the writer František Langer, the historian Josef Šusta, and the political journalist Ferdinand Peroutka. Their meetings helped satisfy Čapek's need for good conversation, and he was expert at drawing out each of his guests. He planted a birch tree in his yard for each of the members; most of these still survive today, though their growth is crowded. Later T. G. Masaryk joined the group, as well as Edvard Beneš. Olga Scheinpflugová says that apparently Masaryk felt a need for lively discussion and found the life of the presidential palace too tame and confining.

Masaryk's friendship brought many attacks on Čapek, both from the right and the left. In spite of his great prestige, Masaryk had many enemies who did not dare to attack him openly, but vented their spite on his friends. The president's favor brought dark references to a "Čapek party" in the press and there was much vicious gossip, some of it published. Though at all times Čapek kept the love and good will of the great majority of his fellow countrymen, he did not fare so well from the nation's press, which took advantage of a weak libel statute to defame him repeatedly.

Matters came to a head at the beginning of 1927. On New Year's Eve, Čapek gave a party which Masaryk attended. A carol by Čapek was performed, a parody of the biblical story of the three wise men; in this case the "wise men" were actually the prime minister, Švehla (later a good friend of Čapek's), the leader of the National Democrats Kramář, and the Slovak Clerical deputy, Hlinka. The National Democratic newspaper *Národ* charged that the performance was politically offensive, and protested against the presence of Masaryk, who is said to have been highly amused. Čapek insisted that it was only a harmless entertainment. To put an end to attacks on him (which were actually veiled attacks on Masaryk), he demanded that *Národ* withdraw its charges. When the newspaper refused, he sued and won the case. The incident inspired him to write a political lampoon, "The Scandalous Affair of Josef Holoušek" (1927), in which he ridiculed the Czech papers' indulgence in rumor-mongering.

The friendship with Masaryk led Čapek to write three volumes of *Conversations with T. G. Masaryk* (1928–35), supplemented after Masaryk's death by an essay, "Silence with T. G. Masaryk" (1935).[29] The *Conversations* were based on long interviews, and Čapek was careful to preserve the informal colloquial tone of Masaryk's speech. He deliberately chose a modest role and his questions on Masaryk's thought are few and succinct; it was not his desire to play Boswell to Masaryk's Johnson. He also insisted that the work should be published under joint authorship, and that half the royalties should go to Masaryk. The publisher finally compromised, and the first edition appeared signed by Čapek's initials only.

Čapek was never primarily interested in politics as such. Still, as he grew older, he came to believe that as a citizen and a writer he had a political responsibility to his nation. His activity as a journalist brought him close to the political sphere. Though he does not seem to have desired any public office for himself, he did take part in an attempt around the middle of the 1920s to found a new liberal party of the professional intelligentsia, the National Labor Party. The new party, which sought support for Masaryk among intellectuals and civil servants, made a poor showing in the 1925 elections.

In the mid-1920s Čapek gave up writing novels and plays almost completely for journalism. To repeated questions as to the reason for his silence he answered, "Now I must help to educate the nation."[30] This reply, which would perhaps seem both condescending and naive in the mouth of a writer and citizen of a great power, can be understood better by one familiar with the psychology of a small nation and its spiritual concerns. Čapek was well able to diagnose the contradictions in the psychology of a small people which had just won its liberation: a sense of inferiority existing side by side with a lack of true humility, professional patriotism without actual sense of national identity, romantic veneration for a dead past without comprehension for real achievements of the present. It was to overcome such weaknesses that he sought to educate his countrymen.

In short, he tried to give them a relativist sense of existence and accomplishment, with an incentive to progress, rather than an unreal, mystical feeling of membership in an absolutist nation or state which could be idealized merely because it was Czechoslovak and not Austro-Hungarian. In accordance with his own *Weltanschauung*, he sought to substitute for an "Austrian" absolutism a new "Czechoslovak" relativism. *Státotvornost* ("state building") was the slogan of Masaryk and the liberals, and Čapek supported their effort. The Czechs, ruled by Austria for centuries, were more accustomed to criticize governments than to support them. The *státotvornost* movement was an effort to educate them to support their own government.

That Čapek might have realized his aim better, in the long run, through creative writing than through journalism, apparently did not occur to him. Irritated by his critics' repeated failure to understand his works, he seemingly gave in to the temptation to speak his mind more directly. His admirers may of course regret that the time he gave to political and didactic writing was not devoted to novels and plays. But in the end Čapek showed that this time had not been wasted; in the middle of this "political" period he suddenly produced the trilogy of novels: *Hordubal* (1933), *Meteor* (1934), and *An Ordinary Life* (1934), which taken together constitute his masterpiece.

In 1932 Čapek published a collection of his more important political essays which had first appeared between 1924 and 1932: *On Public Matters, or Zoon Politikon*. These are "political" in the etymological or broadest sense, however, as the use of the Greek word suggests. Čapek sought to work for the elimination of sharp extremes of right and left in politics. At the same time he strove constantly in his writing to restate political and economic issues as moral ones, questions of right and wrong.[31] Thus, he wrote a number of essays on the problem of poverty and economic justice, which he saw as partly an ethical question, to be solved, if at all, by inspiring a sense of social consciousness in the citizenry as a whole, rather than by radical political or economic reform. He was a socialist, to be sure, though his socialism was vague and he claimed to have no mind for economic questions. He believed in socialization of the means of production, the limitation of the rights of private property, and the control of production and consumption. But his socialism, he stipulated, was rather that of the 1890s, when people were "still carried away by that wave of social action."[32] By this he meant to say, perhaps, that only in his youth could he fully believe the economic myth of the state, that the problem of economic justice can be solved solely by political reform (not to speak of revolution). He never faltered in his opposition to communism, contemporary Czechoslovak and Russian critics to the contrary. Invited to attend May Day, 1938, in Moscow, he refused, though his brother Josef went. His wife reports Čapek to have said at the time that he was accustomed to criticize the countries he visited, and the Soviets would not understand this, for they had no sense of humor. Communist scholars make much of his open letter to *Pravda* welcoming the Soviet constitution of 1936. But in fact his praise of the new constitution was conditional on whether it was actually to be put into practice. His words to this effect were replaced in *Pravda* by a row of dots.[33]

Several times Čapek was a candidate for the Nobel Prize in literature. His enemies even accused him of going to Scandinavia in 1936 to beg for the prize. His wife believes that he did not receive it because his novel, *The War with the Newts* (1936), had made offensive references to Hitler, and the Swedes were loath to risk the loss of good relations with Germany. She writes that he was advised to write a new novel which would "not attack anyone or anything." "Thank you for your good will," he told the intermediary, "but I have already written my doctoral dissertation."

By the mid-1930s Čapek had become acutely aware of the threat posed to Czechoslovak independence by Nazi Germany, and more and more he bent his energies to inspire a will to resist in his countrymen. He carried on an extensive correspondence with Czech leaders, and wrote to foreign writers, urging them to support the Czechoslovak cause. In spite of his strong distaste for speaking on the radio, he made a number of broadcast appeals to his countrymen to unite against the common enemy, as well as an appeal to the Sudeten Germans to discuss their grievances with the Czechoslovaks. He himself came from the Sudeten region of Czechoslovakia, and remembered the communal life of the two peoples as a peaceful one.[34] An admirer once attempted to warn Čapek that his anti-Nazi stand might subject him to personal danger, and pointed out that he was hardly safe at home in his isolated house on the outskirts of Prague. Čapek answered that he was not afraid of hooligans, and that he kept a pistol with which to drive them away. But further questioning revealed that the gun was only a starter's pistol; the gentle Čapek did not wish to hurt anyone, even his attackers.[35]

The Munich settlement of September, 1938, brought a crisis in Čapek's life. His strength had been taxed by his efforts to consolidate the morale of his countrymen and to unite world public opinion against the Germans. No doubt he counted heavily on the British sense of honor and fair play, though his contacts with foreign writers warned him that Britain and France were not spiritually prepared for war. Deeply embittered by the disaster, he wrote a moving

"Greeting" (actually a farewell) to the world. The final paragraph begins with the words:

What can you do, it is terribly far from nation to nation; the further all of us go on, the more we are alone. Now better never set foot outside your homeland; better lock your doors and close your shutters, and let them all do what they like. I no longer care any more what.[36]

But his enemies still had no pity. Anonymous letters denouncing Čapek for his support of the Beneš government arrived at his house. He was abused even on the envelopes themselves, so that the postman was ashamed to deliver them. Rumors appeared in the Agrarian Party papers that he had fled the country; that he had received a secret letter from Beneš before the latter had gone into exile—though neither of these accusations was particularly shameful under the circumstances. A film made of his anti-fascist play, *The White Plague* (1937), was banned by the new regime on its appearance. His wife and many friends besought him to leave Czechoslovakia, where the post-Munich rightist government was hostile to him, and where the menace of German invasion was ever present. But he refused to go.

More than ever Čapek sought to lose himself in his work. He began composing a story called "A Black Hour," about a man who loses everything save his spirit. But he realized that the censorship would not permit its publication, and never finished it. He took up work on a new novel, *The Life and Work of the Composer Foltýn*, which was to serve as a testament of his views on art. It would also strike at his enemies by symbolizing their spiritual impotence in the sterile work of a vain, untalented poseur.

Depressed, and never quite well after Munich, his condition worsened steadily. Finally, after almost a week of illness during which he continued to work, he took to his bed. The doctor's diagnosis was inflammation of both lungs. After two days he seemed a trifle better; he even ate some soup, drank coffee, and smoked his customary half-cigarette. But that afternoon he grew worse. The same evening, on Sunday, Christmas Day, 1938, Karel Čapek died.

It was customary for the funerals of the Czech great to begin at the National Museum, where the body was laid out in state. The Hácha government, fearing a demonstration, brought pressure on the Museum officials to refuse this honor, under the pretext that there was insufficient coal to heat the building. The National Theater likewise refused to sponsor the funeral. The ceremony was arranged privately, and Čapek was buried at Vyšehrad, the resting place of the Czech immortals. The petition of a group of students and workers who asked permission to line the streets during the procession was denied. In spite of the threat of official disfavor, however, the people who loved him packed the streets along the entire line of the procession.

Čapek's most expressive epitaph was perhaps the one written by Shaw, who said:

It is too absurd. It should have been my turn this time. Karel was far too young to go like that. He had at least another forty years to give so much to the world. His plays proved him to be a prolific and terrific playwright.[37]

On March 15, 1939, Nazi troops entered Prague. A house-to-house search for political opponents at once began. Hurriedly Čapek's widow destroyed his extensive correspondence, which might have involved others; there was no time to separate the innocuous from the incriminating, and almost everything perished. Soon the Gestapo agents, still unaware of Čapek's death three months before, arrived to arrest him.

Josef Čapek was arrested and taken to a concentration camp. He died in Bergen-Belsen, probably of typhus, only a few weeks before the end of the war. Thus, in a sense, he continued to play his role of protector, enduring as proxy the agony which his younger brother had been spared.

2. Back to Someone

When the Brothers Čapek made their literary debut in 1908, the reigning literary currents in Bohemia were realism and symbolism. Realism, and its offspring, naturalism, dominated Czech fiction. The realist movement, with its roots primarily in French and Russian fiction, had come belatedly to Bohemia, and still commanded a serious reception among the Czech intelligentsia. But the literary avant-garde, and particularly the poets, had already discarded realism for symbolism. Czech symbolism developed largely under the influence of Western writers, especially of Whitman, Baudelaire, Oscar Wilde, Verlaine, Verhaeren, Maeterlinck, and later Rimbaud. Much of Czech symbolist poetry was derivative, but several poets did succeed in achieving real originality and profundity, as well as new heights of euphony in their verse; among these are Otokar Březina (1868–1929) and Antonín Sova (1864–1928).

As elsewhere in Europe, the label "symbolist" denoted a number of diverse trends. Both Březina, with his rhapsodic faith in a pantheistic cosmos, and Sova, with his quietist contemplation and his visions of a vague but better future, were life-asserting in their poetry. Though at times they lapsed into melancholy and even despair, they made their poetry a vehicle for expression of new, personal faiths.

A second group of Czech symbolists preferred to cultivate the "flowers of evil" of decadence. Inspired by Baudelaire, Wilde, and Huysmans, they sought escape in illusions, erotic dreams, and in a cult of social nihilism; they indulged in fantasies of demonism and perverse love. The leader of this camp was Jiří Karásek ze Lvovic (1871–1951). Around 1905, Karásek and his followers ranged around the journal *Moderní revue*, passed from "decadence" to so-called "neo-romanticism." The neo-romantics created a prose fiction of exotic and mysterious atmosphere, an artificial, poetized style, and frequent use of the apparatus of the supernatural.

The situation in Czech literature between 1905 and 1910 was dynamic and fluid. The younger generation of beginning writers was already growing dissatisfied with symbolism and decadence. The decadent poets turned in a restricted circle of themes and ideas which very quickly grew stale. But there was no question of a return to realism, which was also the achievement of an older generation. For a short time Karásek's neo-romanticism served as a compromise, and most of those who began writing around 1910 adhered to the school briefly. But these younger writers were scanning the wider European horizon, seeking new schools and slogans which could rescue them from passive imitation of the older literary tradition.

Czech literary historians later called this generation the "pragmatist generation," or simply the "Čapek generation."[1] The first term emphasizes the influence of the pragmatist philosophers and of Bergson on the younger writers. Indeed, foreign philosophical influences were at first more noticeable in their work than any purely literary ones, as Čapek later observed.[2] In spite of the initial strong influence of optimistic philosophical trends, the "pragmatist generation" was destined very soon to become a spiritually "lost generation" in Czech literature. World War I disbanded its members at the very moment when they were emerging as a coherent movement.[3] As for foreign literary influences, the "pragmatists" found an almost embarrassing variety in post-impressionist movements such as futurism, unanimism, and expressionism. This diversity of influence also helped to blur the clear lines of their artistic personality. Hence it is more difficult to characterize this generation than either the one which preceded it, or the younger generation which came after it. It was a generation which preferred prose to poetry, though poetry had always been dominant in the older Czech tradition, and became so again with the younger generation of the 1920s. It was a generation which entered literature under the standard of the avant-garde, but later settled down to relative conservatism. Finally, the pragmatists created (in the work of the Brothers Čapek and František Langer) the first Czech drama which enjoyed any success outside Bohemia.

The first tendency from abroad which seemed to offer something new to these young writers was German neo-classicism, led by Paul Ernst. Ernst taught that literary art consists in the creation of closed, precise forms. The two ideal forms of literature for him were the Greek tragedy in drama, and the Italian Renaissance *novella* in fiction. Narration in fiction should be restricted to bare action, motivated by character or by fate, but kept free of psychological analysis. Doubtless Ernst was influenced in his Italian preferences by the trip he made to Italy in 1900, but the vogue for Italy took root in Bohemia as well, and around 1910 young Czech writers such as František Khol (1877–1930), František Langer (1888–), and the Brothers Čapek, were studiously reproducing an Italian atmosphere they had never seen. At first sight neo-classicism seemed tempting, for it provided a formal discipline which both symbolism and realism lacked: symbolism in its impressionism of technique, its fondness for rhapsodic improvization; realism in its formless accumulation of detail. At the same time the exotic setting of Renaissance Italy and the preference for motifs of erotic love and intrigue, typical of Ernst's tales, coincided with the neo-romantic tastes of the home school. But the neo-classical trend very soon proved sterile, for it provided no new content, only form. In the work of the Brothers Čapek, its influence is obvious only in the stories which they published in the early part of 1910.

In the years 1912–14, two new foreign poetic currents made themselves felt almost simultaneously in Czech literature. The first of these was Italian futurism, with its rejection of past tradition and its glorification of sensual experience, of civilization and modern urban life. And from France there came unanimism, exemplified in the early novels of Jules Romains and the poetry of Duhamel, Vildrac, and many others. The unanimists, following the sociology of Durkheim, to which they gave a mystical cast, preached the doctrine of a collective soul. It was the writer's task, they insisted, to depict this collective soul in a new humanistic literature concerned with the masses.

These trends had almost no direct followers as such in Czech literature, but they did inspire the development of a native Czech school—vitalism. Vitalism celebrated the joys of human existence: nature, sexual love, and intoxication with life. Philosophically, of course, the movement reflected Bergson's doctrine of the *élan vital*. The Czech vitalists idealized primitive life as more natural and spontaneous than civilized life, and contended that art must recapture this lost primitive spirit.

Vitalist tendencies are evident in the stories which the Brothers Čapek published in 1911 and 1912, as well as in the few poems which Karel wrote in this early period. But at the end of 1912, in their story, "The Luminous Depths," the brothers lost the spontaneous joy in life reflected so exuberantly in their early writing, and were suddenly brought face to face with the contradiction and tragedy of human existence. The war years confirmed them in the sense of life's horror, and only several years after the end of the war was Karel able to reassert something of the earlier unanimist and vitalist spirit. *R.U.R.* (1920), with its concern for the fate of humanity and its faith in the ultimate triumph of life and love, shows unanimist and vitalist influences. Something of the unamimist idealization of the collective also survives in Čapek's later novel, *The First Rescue Party* (1937). And the admiration for the primitive always remained with him, expressed not only in his fondness for folk art, but also in his distrust of modern technology and nostalgia for a simple, contented life lived close to nature. But this, of course, was very far from the primitive "barbarism" of Marinetti and the futurists.

In 1913 the younger generation made its formal debut in the *Almanac for the Year 1914*. In the nineteenth century younger Czech writers had frequently banded together to publish an almanac. The new generation poked fun at this tradition, even printing a calendar to parody the almanac form. Besides the two Brothers Čapek, the volume contained writing by S. K. Neumann (1875–1947), an older decadent who had joined forces with the younger poets, Otokar

Fischer (1883–1938), Arne Novák (1880–1939), and Otakar Theer (1880–1917). Karel contributed but one short poem to the almanac; still its appearance is important for his development, since the almanac was the first (and ultimately the only) manifestation of the unity of a coming generation with which, at the time, he identified himself closely.

Čapek himself has left one of the best characterizations of the ideology of the writers who launched the almanac.[4] Vitalism was the chief new trend which inspired their work. But their program was largely negative, Čapek observes. They rejected impressionism, symbolism, decadence, in fact, all subjectivism. They attempted to use language concretely and precisely, cutting words away from the connotative associations the symbolist poets had given them. The positive program of the young group was philosophical rather than literary. The reigning philosophical school among the older Czech writers, especially the symbolists, was neo-Kantian idealism, with its faith in super-personal, absolute values; its leading exponent in literature was the critic F. X. Šalda (1867–1937). The younger generation, led by Neumann, was influenced rather by Bergsonian vitalism, pragmatism, and activism. To the cult of absolute values these writers opposed a relativist metaphysics and ethics, with emphasis on the freedom of the individual personality and action in terms of the concrete situation.

Cubism had a strong influence on the pragmatist generation, and early cubist painting had already made a strong impression on the brothers during their stay in Paris in 1911. Josef returned to Prague to paint in a modified cubist style, while both brothers wrote articles in defense of the new painting and its esthetics. Karel even announced at the time that he considered himself a "literary cubist." In this he was not a follower of Apollinaire and his school (who also used the term); rather he attempted to apply the theory of cubism directly to his own writing. The focal point of art for Čapek is not the artist and his expression, but the objective work of art he creates, which is no mere representation, but a creative reconstruction of reality. In this process the artist may analyze, dissect, and distort, as the cubist painter refracts the image into a series of planes; he may produce a finished result which corresponds to no given reality, yet which will be valid in itself and at the same time true to a deeper reality, to an essence or Platonic idea.

Cubist theory was the strongest single influence on Čapek's esthetics, and cubism provided him with an artistic formula for expressing his relativist attitude towards truth. The multiplicity of the planes of a cubist painting correspond to the diversity of points of view from which different observers perceive the same reality. From 1917 on most of Čapek's novels, plays, and stories illustrate this relativism, or, in its more sophisticated form, perspectivism. In his novel *Meteor* (1934), he achieves something very close to "cubism" in literature: the reconstruction of the life of an unknown man from the testimonies of a number of observers who employ different forms of cognition: scientific observation, deduction, induction, intuition, and artistic inspiration. The result is not the image of the unknown man, or of any man, for that matter—this is impossible—but rather an image which is *human* and true to man's actual essence.

German expressionism, both in literature and in painting, is the last of these influences which should be mentioned. Literary expressionism is an extreme form of subjectivism: the artist distorts reality in his need to express and at the same time objectify his deepest inner feelings. Like cubism, expressionism focused attention on the created work of art as a concrete fact. But it was also a reflection, an embodiment of subjective reality *within* the artist. The cubists stressed perception rather than feeling, and argued that art was a representation of the essences of objects rather than their subjective meaning to any one observer.

In this opposition Čapek sided with the cubists. He detested the theory of art as self-expression, which for him seemed a monstrous piece of presumption. Art is the creation of objective facts, he insisted, though in practice, and even in theory, he was not always able to rule the self-expressive element out entirely. It is interesting that he ignored the French fauvist painters almost completely in his early reviews and articles on modern painting, though he must certainly have seen their work during his stay in Paris in 1911. Fauvist esthetics were likewise subjective, and had a strong influence on the German expressionists.

Josef Čapek was influenced by expressionism, however, and this theoretical split may well be the reason for the end of the brothers' collaboration in 1912. From that time Josef's writing proceeded further in the direction of distortion and an agonized lyricism, passing almost into surrealism, while Karel emphasized cognitive qualities in his art, such as point of view, observation, and analysis.

Curiously enough, in his later work (beginning with *R.U.R.*) Karel did not object to using expressionist techniques in his plays and fantastic novels. In many respects he was an eclectic, eager for experimentation with new forms and genres. His literary practice was often at variance with his theory.

Čapek's doctoral dissertation, accepted by Charles University in 1915, treated the theme of "Objective Methods in Esthetics." In contemporary German philosophy he found theoretical support for the objective status of the work of art. At the same time German estheticians such as Max Dessoir, Konrad Fiedler, and Emil Utitz called for the psychological study of the processes of artistic creation and perception. Čapek grudgingly admitted the validity of psychological research in esthetics, but did not stress the psychological approach, which could easily have led back to a total subjectivism (and historically did in fact foreshadow the rise of expressionism). Rather he emphasized the possibility of objective criticism and history of art; here he followed such estheticians as Ernst Grosse and August Schmarsow: the critic should study the genesis of art forms, their historical development, and their interrelations. Art itself cannot progress, Čapek observed at the close of the dissertation. We cannot say that art today is better than it was a thousand years ago; it is simply different. But the "science of art" does progress; only in modern times has it been possibile to write the history of art. At the same time our perceptions become keener and our analyses more subtle. Art criticism is a modern discipline, which scarcely existed a few centuries ago. In spite of its relatively short life, it has made phenomenal strides. The variety and divergence of critical points of view only proves the subtlety and refinement of analysis we have achieved. Čapek's dissertation is not very original (it is less interesting than his articles on art of the same period), but it does illustrate his strong revulsion against all forms of romanticist and impressionist subjectivism; to these he opposes esthetic objectivism and pluralism (the variety of forms of art and of artistic experience, as contrasted to their uniqueness).

In 1913 Čapek published his first translations of modern French poetry. During the war years he continued to translate to show his sympathy for the French cause, though nothing was published during these years. Ultimately in 1920 a volume appeared, *Modern French Poetry*, containing ninety-five poems by fifty-two poets from Baudelaire to the postwar period. A second edition, with fourteen new poems, appeared in 1936. Čapek's translations had almost incalculable significance for the development of modern Czech poetry. Though most of the younger Czech poets could read French verse in the original and were influenced by it, they were unable to create a new Czech poetic form and style adequate to the new sensibility. Čapek threw over the traditional style and artificial sentence order which had dominated Czech verse since the 1870s, and which is characteristic of his own earlier writing, both in verse and prose. For these he substituted a new lexicon, stripped of ornament and intrinsic pathos, and a new, simpler, and more natural sentence structure in which the rhythmic effect was freer and relied more on intonation than on regularity of stress.

This free verse style, paradoxically, saw little use in Čapek's own work, since he wrote almost no poetry in later life. But the exercise in translation had its value, for it demonstrated the futility of the artificial, decorative style he and his brother had cultivated in early youth. From the end of the war he strove constantly to find more natural forms of expression. His failure to write lyric poetry he ascribed to modesty: he was reluctant to express his ego directly, but had to take refuge behind the characters of drama or fiction.

From the beginning of their literary career, the brothers published reviews of art and literature, as well as articles on a variety of subjects. A long review of Růžena Svobodová's collection of stories, *The Sacred Spring* (1912),[5] provided Karel with an opportunity to polemicize with the symbolists. He criticizes Svobodová for her romantic fatalism, her artificial psychology, for decorative estheticism, and for an artificial cult of the primitive. But for the most part he was interested in new trends rather than older ones. He was the first in Bohemia to review French writers such as Apollinaire[6] and

Jules Romains,[7] to give a theoretical justification of free verse, and to write on cubist painting[8] and the beginnings of German expressionism.[9] He was first to describe and criticize the sociology of Durkheim.[10] An early article by the brothers on the film is of interest; they stress its almost "satanic precision" and technical perfection, its vividness as compared with the stage. They predict that the theater will abandon spectacle to the film, and itself attempt to appeal more directly to feeling.[11] Karel has an amusing article on literary eroticism in which he observes that the erotic character of a writer's work is not necessarily connected with his sexual life; an increase in the erotic character of his writing may not necessarily coincide with an increase in his sexual activity.[12]

Among Čapek's many reviews, there is one of Woodrow Wilson's *Mere Literature* (in German translation); this is in fact a discussion of American philosophy of life. Though later Čapek was to grow distrustful of America as a land of materialist technology, here he is glowing in his praise. America's practical spirit, her technology, her activism—all these are sorely needed in Europe, he declares, especially in Bohemia. America has found in pragmatism a philosophical expression for her new spirit. Europeans call pragmatism a "business man's philosophy," but fail to realize that still it *is* a philosophy; Europeans act without philosophy. In fact America has realized a new synthesis:

a harmonic equilibrium of thought and action, of spirit and its elaboration in activity. The progress in which the American, who is typically a non-conservative, believes, is animated by spirit, not by the feverish battle of *arrivisme*, by culture, not tricks, by knowledge, not money. This is the real example which America provides, and which Europe overlooks.[13]

3. Spring Improvisations

The short pieces which the Brothers Čapek published between 1908 and 1912 may well seem alien and remote for us today. This a partly because they were written in a period of literary transition, but partly also because they are on the periphery of literary art itself. One scarcely knows today how to define many of these pieces in terms of genre: as causeries, sketches, feuilletons, epigrams, or what. They seem to be related more closely to the society which produced them than to the stream of literature as such. And hence they arouse in us something of that sense of the exotic which advertisements or popular prints and drawings of the period might bring.

This does not mean, however, that these early pieces lack real literary merit. On the contrary, if we compare them to their proto-types in Viennese journalism—to the anecdotes and epigrams of such writers as Peter Altenberg or Roda-Roda—we can only con-firm the originality of the brothers' work. Their pieces have more of the wonder and intoxication of life; they are more exuberant and outrageous. With all their apparent sophistication, they are clearly the work of young, ingenuous spirits whose view of life is still flexible and unbiased. With their lack of evident form and discipline, they are clearly literary beginnings.

In 1918 the brothers collected and reprinted more than half of their early pieces under the title of *The Garden of Krakonoš*. To the volume they added an autobiographical preface, in its way the best thing in the collection. The book's title refers to the mountain land in which the brothers were born and reared; the "garden" of the fantastic giant Krakonoš is in the valley of the river Úpa, surrounded by high mountains. The soil is blood-red, and there are great boulders which resemble idols. But the reference seems little more than a catchy image; none of the pieces is set in this "garden," nor have their sensual fantasies any connection with the boys' homeland or the legends of the fairy-tale giant. It is the decadent cities of Central Europe of the day which form the background of most of the pieces: Prague, Vienna, Berlin. In fact, the introductory self-portrait corresponds rather to the brothers' mood in 1918, when each independently was making his actual début as a serious writer. In 1908 they had not really committed themselves to literature, and still showed a curious, almost naive indifference to a literary reputation. Though the public speculated as to their identity, they preferred to maintain an air of mystery. There were rumors that "Brothers Čapek" was only a pseudonym for a ruined broker, a "man with a past," or an unknown Frenchman whose pieces were translated for the Prague journals. Karel Horký's *Stopa* published a light-hearted footnote: "In answer to numerous inquiries as to the identity of our two contributors who write under the name of the Brothers Čapek, we wish to inform the public that one is Matěj K. Čapek of *Národní listy,* and the other Kubata, who lost his head for Blata."[1] "Matěj K. Čapek" was Karel Matěj Čapek, a distinguished Czech novelist of the naturalist school, who also wrote for the newspaper *Národní listy.* (Later, while a colleague of Karel Čapek's on that paper, he added the appellative Chod to his last name to distinguish himself from his younger namesake.) "Kubata who lost his head for Blata" is the hero of a popular Czech ballad; this reference was pure nonsense.

The autobiographical preface to *The Garden of Krakonoš,* in its way the freshest and most charming piece in the volume, sheds much light on the mentality of two young men who were considering devoting themselves to literature:

How did you do it? So far we are ignorant of how the two Goncourts worked together, or the Rosnys, or of how librettists work. The authors of these pieces went in for literature very early, it is true, and in a state of complete literary savagery. They were not even aware that to write together is something out of the ordinary. They came from the country, where they had grown up together; they had no friends in Prague, and thus could turn only to each other. They wrote together because it seemed easier to them, and because neither had confidence in himself. When later they were obliged to supply the newspapers each week with an article, it was their practice to decide jointly, quickly, and without hesitation, what they should write. They found their impulse to write most often while reading the papers, in current events, changes of season and of weather; the form was supplied by their ignorance and youth.

At that time the authors did not even realize what a strange and eccentric impression their pieces had on the public...

Literary influences. If the authors were to admit frankly to the literary influences which they have undergone, that is, the books which they liked the most, they would reveal the narrow range of their reading at the time. No doubt they read the things which were then corrupting all the youth: the fascinating eyes of Jarry's Messalina intoxicated them, and they were enchanted by Wilde's Salomé and Dorian Gray; they were impressed by Strindberg, Hamsun and Garborg, and later by Stendahl; they knew Poe, Baudelaire, and Huysmans—in a word, everything that anyone ignorant of foreign languages could read in translation. But Hlaváček, Neumann, and Dyk [Czech decadent poets of the period] also spoke to them in those days; may they pardon us for listing them in this connection.

And Prague. Life itself. Before the authors could recover from their first amazement at the grandeur of a metropolis, their first intoxication at its sensual luxury, their first astonishment at its (seemingly) immense vistas which its electric artificialty projected onto the blank screen of their world, it was too late—this book had already been written. And so it contained much lyric enchantment as well as curious taste, eccentric gaudiness, harsh black-and-white illumination, love of vulgarity, joy in innovation, and pleasure in the world.

Critics like to aim straight at the "target" of an author's literary influences, and authors are given to reacting with disgust when thus—on purpose—the ground is cut out from under their feet. To the brothers it has even happened more than once that cursory criticism has ascribed to their work "influences of Spanish, Italian, French, English and American literatures," unfortunately most often without listing a more detailed bibliography, so that if true, the two would have been the most unoriginal and least talented authors in Bohemia. But this is a distinction which they are too modest to claim. Rather they now republish their older pieces as evidence of what they were actually worth as writers.

The astral influence of Venus is undoubtedly to be found in this book. As for literary influences, the authors would be pleasantly surprised if anyone (with good intentions) should find intelligent and famous godfathers for these first fruits of literary savagery from which only later did they slowly awaken.

Their later life has little to do with this book. After the collection comes a series of events, travels, occupations, and interests; if to some the path of their literary development has seemed crooked, it is much less crooked and illogical than the road of life itself. Only it seems equally true that early youth sees much badly and out of all proportions, with an awe and wonderment that magnifies and distorts; only after youth passes does there come a time of attentiveness to things, of more humble watching and listening. Early youth feels obscurely the plurality and mystery of life, and surmounts it with a valiant ardor and a fantasy projected into the unknown; only later does man learn to observe, at times with trembling and anxiety. Therefore do not seek in this book for that which cannot be found in it. It is a book of early youth, of twenty years of age...

He who wants to strike a dog can always find a cane. And, on the other hand, he who wants to pet him can always find a kind word. Here, for anyone who wants to use them, are a few *canes:* an immature book, frivolous, artificial, full of purely intellectual wit, un-Czech, conceited, decadent, paradoxical, light, unnatural, superficial, *passé.* And here—for anyone who wants—a few *friendly* words: an immature book, lyrical, spirited, naive, fresh, wistful and wild.

This final paragraph expresses much of the paradoxical character of the collection. In fact, the pieces *are* decadent, and sometimes even crude in their eroticism, yet they are also naive, fresh, and outrageous, and poke fun at the extravagances of decadence. Eroticism is the favored theme; the pieces are replete with an atmosphere of demonic women, tropical winds, and "onanistic monkeys." Every stylized conception of love is represented: love as sensual pleasure, as compulsive slavery, as the eternal, monotonous cycle of falling in and out of love. Only real, mature love is absent. This is deliberate, and no cynical pose; it is not that the brothers doubt the reality of real love, but they are well aware that it is not a suitable subject for their urbane satire.

There are many epigrams on love, sex, and woman, some witty, others banal:

God created man in His own image and woman in the image of life. Man is God in miniature; hence he creates. Woman is nature in miniature; hence she gives birth.

"A woman is no more than a body." Empty-headed cynic, how can you overlook her toilette?

The sins of youth are an assurance of a contented old age, for they give old age something to remember.

The tears of women are a Lethe, from which they drink oblivion; a cup from which they become drunk; a bath, in which they are purified; a moat, with which they defend themselves against enemies; a well, in which they look conceitedly for a reflection of their virtue; last of all, they are water, which flows.

Man loves in woman all that is created: nature and human being, clay and stars, perfume, life, and all that is created; woman loves in man all that is not created: longing and chimera, dream and idea, and all that is not created.

"I am for educating women. A woman should be as intellectual as possible. Woman should be the spiritual equal of man. Woman should be cultured."

"Madame, that would be too bad for woman, for then man whould understand her."

An unequal battle: if woman does not give in, she is victor; if she does, she dictates the conditions of her conquest; in both cases she wins.

The eroticism of the collection is an eroticism which intentionally parodies itself. The sketch entitled "Olga Desmond" burlesques the nudity of a Berlin cabaret dancer. Her nakedness is an eloquent lesson to remind us that we are all "temples of God and that the Holy Spirit rests in us." Yet even her nudity falls short of the ideal, for she has but two breasts; a more authentic goddess would be the Phrygian Diana, with her sixteen mammary glands.

In "Marriage" a wife complains of the sexual indignities she is continually forced to bear at the hands of her husband. The brothers advise the husband never to give up the role of the young lover; throughout marriage he should go on proffering blushes and fair speeches; at the same time he should never abandon the passion of brutality and assault.

This paradoxical duality in the lover's treatment of his beloved leads to the paradox of woman as a being whom man regards, on one hand, as purely physical; on the other, as ideal and spiritual. Man corrupts woman by creating her in the image he desires for her. The final result of this corruption is the demonic woman, a projection of the needs of masochistic man. The type is illustrated in "Carnival in Venice," in the person of the sadistic Countess Tarnovská, the heroine of a contemporary scandal who induced two of her lovers to murder a third.

The image of the demonic woman is one of the imprints with which decadence has marked the brothers' work. Another is their utterly artificial style, influenced by the poetic language of Vrchlický and the Czech symbolists, rich in inversions, participial phrases, and in archaic expressions and images. This artificiality of style is partly the result of the youth of the two authors, partly of the uncertainty in standards of a transitional period. But it is also an exaggeration which moves toward parody. In fact, some of the earliest of the pieces, such as the erotic sketches described above, are parodies of decadence itself. "A Famous Man" (1908) is a burlesque of the figure of the decadent hero, whose chief claim to greatness is his mysteriousness. "The Abominable Loves of Moren" (1908) concerns a young man who loves only ugly or grotesque women; on the long list of his former loves are a dead woman, a Negress with huge lips, and a member of a pair of Siamese twins who lacked one leg.[2] In "A Fatal Supper" (1909) a band of sophisticates rattle off brittle epigrams on love and death, and the latter, conjured up by their talk, strikes down one of their number.

Though this kind of ridicule and parody is an important quality of these early pieces, the sense of the collection is not limited to parody alone. The first two of the three pieces mentioned in the foregoing paragraph were not even reprinted by the brothers when they came to assemble *The Garden of Krakonoš*. Not parody, but satire is important for the young authors. Some of this satire, as in "Wheat" or "Argentine Meat," is purely topical, a reaction to newspaper headlines of the day. A transition from this topical satire to a more sweeping social criticism is found in "Unemployment" (1909). After describing real scenes of poverty brought on by unemployment, the brothers move on in an almost dadaist spirit to fantastic associations of the idea of "unemployment": a nobleman whose mistress has thrown him over is now "unemployed," as are the army officers who long for war, or the Sphinx, now that her riddle is solved. The frivolity of these associations hardly destroys the real social criticism of the earlier scenes; presumably what the brothers were seeking was a heightening of effect by contrasting real poverty with effeteness.

An element of utopian fantasy is combined with satire in several of these pieces. In "The Pleasures of the Moment," the brothers defend pleasure against the charge that it is of trifling worth just because it is fleeting. Suppose that a machine could be invented which would prolong pleasure; then its short duration could no longer be a legitimate objection. This suggestion for a hedonistic utopia anticipates Huxley's *Brave New World*. The best example of utopian satire, however, is found in one of the brothers' very first pieces, "The System" (1908). An American capitalist maintains a model factory where the workers are kept under the strictest spiritual control. All pastimes, displays of emotion, or pursuits of the spirit are rigorously excluded from their ken. Each worker lives exactly like every other one; even his dreams, induced by controlled stimuli, are the same. Sexual contacts are limited to prescribed occasions, and then all light is excluded, so that the worker can never perceive beauty and romantically idealize his experience. But on one occasion a supervisor forgets to extinguish a light, and a worker acquires a sense of beauty and refinement from his erotic experience, and his deepest emotions are stirred. This discovery leads to a revolt of feelings among the workers. In the end they destroy the factory and murder their employer's wife and three children. This paradox of savage violence stemming from "loftier feelings" is a burlesque, of course, but it also recalls Nietzsche or Dostoevski. The theme of the dehumanization of man as the price of modern technological civilization was later used by Karel Čapek in *R.U.R.* and *The War with the Newts*.

The same fear of dehumanization is clearly expressed in "The Unit." A man's whole significance for modern society lies in statistical definition; what is important is not his individuality, but the number of larger social groups to which he belongs. But the unit is little more than zero, and a number, no matter how large, times zero is still zero; without qualitative significance, quantity cannot avail man much.

The pieces are a collection of paradoxes: the human and the mechanical; spiritual and sexual love; woman as goddess and as purely physical being. It is the first of these paradoxes which rings truest in the brothers' treatment. Indeed, the collection as a whole can be read as an implicit plea for naturalness in a decadent world infected with the artificiality of civilization. The authors only pretend to accept the sophistication of the world about them; actually for them whatever is artificial is sterile. A short piece called "Artificial Flowers" expresses this conviction:

Artificial flowers are made as follows: from papers saturated with artificial pigments, and from wires which will prick your palms, from these papers and wires delicate creations can be made, which in fact resemble flowers. Do you want to have the illusion of a bouquet torn off with bare hands? You will not have it. Hence artificial flowers will not help you recall the beauty of nature; you will do better if you think of a young flower-girl, who too is extremely artificial, as she glances nervously up from her fine work. This pretty flower-girl is currently in love with a frivolous gentleman who comes to see her only in the evenings; and she is falling victim to nervous ennui. During attacks of this ailment she devises new forms for her blossoms, pamphlet-like rather than truly botanic. These are what artificial flowers are like.

In the widest sense, artificial flowers are made only from paper and the restless movements of fine hands which feel themselves deserted.

With its *recherché* manner, *The Garden of Krakonoš* shows little connection with the brothers' later work. Still there is a close thematic unity between these youthful pieces and their subsequent writing. Indeed, the conflict of nature and civilization within man was to become Karel Čapek's most significant theme. Several of the last pieces prefigure specific later developments in the brothers' work. Thus, "Carnival in Venice" and "Spring Improvisation" or "A Lunar Comedy" have something of the surrealist quality of

Josef's later writing. A kind of lyrical philosophizing foreshadows Karel's *Wayside Crosses*. The piece called "Time" forms a bridge to that collection:

Among the cruelest punishments which justice commands today is solitary confinement: a room, loneliness, and twenty-four hours; for twenty-four hours a man is set face to face with time, and he leaves the cell in which he has confronted time crushed and listless. For solitary confinement is the torment of time.

And time is suffering and endurance.

4. Ex Centro; or The Fateful Game of Love

Until 1910, the brothers had written little narrative fiction. The few stories they had published are brief, slight in form, and journalistic in tone. The neo-classical tale of Paul Ernst, which was then coming into vogue in Bohemia,[1] provided a ready form for longer narratives, and early in 1910 the brothers published two tales in the new manner, with the customary Italianesque setting.[2] Though the tales were successful, the authors were presumably aware of the derivative character of their new neo-classical form, and soon abandoned it.

The first of these stories, "The Red Tale," is set in the early nineteenth-century Italy of the Carbonari, though its mood and atmosphere are more typical of the Renaissance. The tale is told by one of the guests at a fashionable club party. Before he tells his story, however, an extravagant scene in the style of *The Garden of Krakonoš* takes place. The banqueteers exchange brittle epigrams, while another guest, "young Richard," disappointed in love, excuses himself discreetly to go off to shoot himself. This narrative frame serves not so much to motivate the telling of the story as to provide an ironic atmosphere for the love tale that follows. It also makes an ironic contrast between the past of the tale proper and the present of the frame: in past times men killed each other for love; now they kill themselves.

The tale proper concerns the rivalry of two men in love with the same girl. They fight a duel, masked and dressed in similar costumes. One is killed. The girl mistakenly supposes that her lover is the victor, and joyously declares that she loves only him, and that she despised the dead man. Silently the other accepts her passionate kisses. When his mask is removed his face is so covered with wounds that the girl still mistakes his identity. The two live passionately as lovers. But slowly she begins to suspect the truth, and finally one morning he is found dead, his newly healed wounds burst open. The girl goes back to the convent in which she had been reared, to lose herself again in her former sensual love for Jesus.

The second tale, "L'Éventail," is more sophisticated. Set at the end of the eighteenth century, the atmosphere is again that of the Renaissance *novella*. An Italian prince gives a garden fete. There his mistress flirts openly with a poet, and later in the evening the prince comes upon the two and catches them *in flagrante*. A puppet show is to be staged, and the director has brought a beautiful female puppet which mechanically pronounces the words *si* and *no* in regular alternation. Masked, the prince appears on the stage in a dialogue with the puppet, to interrogate it on the fidelity of women. The contradictory answers of the puppet enrage him, and he rushes off into the darkness. Suddenly a terrific thunderstorm bursts; as the guests hasten to leave, they see the prince chasing after the poet with drawn sword; later they pass the body of the dead poet.

The puppet of the tale serves as a symbol of the eternal enigma of the feminine, which man can never fathom. Indeed, her alternate answers of *si* and *no* suggest the relativity of all truth, appearing to man as arbitrary and contradictory. Love is viewed as a paradox or accident of fate (as in "The Red Tale"), which, when pursued, only reveals the endless contradictions of human nature and the enigma of woman.

The two tales are told in a light, ironic tone, which dissociates the authors' sympathies from the characters. The tendency (particularly apparent in "L'Éventail") to break up the action into slight, anecdotal scenes, strung together by ironic commentary, unites these tales with the pieces of *The Garden of Krakonoš*. While these stories are not exactly parodies, it is clear that the authors had no intention of identifying themselves with neo-classicism; for them it was little more than a school of technique. The break with Ernst's teachings was to become evident in their next work.

In 1910 the brothers also wrote a one-act comedy, *The Fateful Game of Love*. The play is a modern, ironic treatment of the characters and situations of the *commedia dell'arte*. Since the Italian *commedia* was a traditional source of symbolist imagery (Jules La Forgue, Verlaine, etc.), it is possible to view the play as another parody of symbolism and decadence. The idea of a modern *commedia dell'arte* was in the air at the time; Rudolf Lothar's popular *König Harlequin* (1900) and Alexander Blok's "pierrotic comedy," *Balagančik* (*The Sideshow*, 1907) are two prior examples. There were also earlier romantic essays in the genre, such as Théophile Gautier's *Pierrot posthume* (1847), or Leoncavallo's opera *I Pagliacci* (1892), in which a *commedia dell'arte* performance is staged. But there were not many such models, and in retrospect the Čapeks' conception seems quite original: to expose the artificiality of stage conventions by parodying an established theatrical form. It is at least possible that the idea occurred to them as the logical result of Ernst's neo-classical teachings and their own experience with the Italian tales. In the drama Ernst favored Greek tragedy. If his ideas were applied to comedy, however, the classical form of the comedy might well be the Italian *commedia*. Born in the Renaissance, it could trace its lineage back to Roman comedy. But *The Fateful Game of Love* is not, of course, a serious example of neo-classicism. Ernst accepted the forms he chose as self-contained and self-justifying, while the Brothers Čapek use the form and its conventions to ridicule and expose the very forms and conventions of the theater itself. Hence, the play becomes a kind of parody of neo-classicism, and the real close of the neo-classical episode in their writing.

In their parody the brothers also hit at the cult of illusionism in symbolist literature. They tear off the masks of their characters, exposing their self-deceptions. Scaramouche is a "real madman, and no mere mask." The romantic Gilles's sensitivity and physical weakness are diagnosed by the doctor as caused by "love, dancing and self-abuse." The heroine, Isabella, is introduced by the Prologue quite bluntly as "woman"; she serves only to motivate the intrigue. Brighella drives the rival suitors to a frenzy by lifting Isabella's skirts in their presence. When this is done, he tells her that she may go, for her "role is played." Love appears as an illusion which serves merely to clothe animal passion, and the lifting of Isabella's skirts reminds us forcibly of the appearance of the naked heroine at the duel in "The Red Tale"; both scenes serve chiefly to motivate the violence of the coming action.

The content of the play is slight enough. Brighella schemes to involve the two rival suitors, Gilles and Trivalin, in a duel, so that he can run off with their money and with Isabella. Unlike a true *commedia*, the text of the play is fixed, of course, but the impression is constantly given that the actors are improvising. The characters wear modern dress. The Prologue begins by speaking in verse, but Gilles interrupts in prose, and refuses to speak verse even when the Prologue reminds him that it belongs to his part. From then on the actors speak in verse or prose, depending on the nature of the scene and the character of their parts. The verse is iambic pentameter with varying rhyme patterns. The liveliest parts of the play are those in which the actors poke fun at the conventions of the stage themselves. The doctor asks the public why it has come to see the actors' art: even if the actors play as best they are able, the public will only think that they are real people and forget that they are actors. Evil is better than good on the stage, Brighella observes, for it serves to motivate the plot. Scaramouche reminds the spectators that while they are amusing themselves, their wives at home may be deceiving them and their servants reading their letters. During a love scene Scaramouche tells the public that the theater is on fire, so that it will leave and the lovers may be left to themselves.

In spite of the play's freshness and wit, its publication went almost unnoticed. Indeed, it remained unperformed until the mid-1920s, when a small theater in Prague presented it. On May 15, 1930, it had its official première, but then only in the Studio of the National Theater as part of an evening of one-act plays. No doubt it was ahead of its time for Czech literature. The Czech public was as yet unused to symbolist theater, which it knew chiefly from the imitative fairy plays of Jaroslav Kvapil (1868–1950). Hence it was scarcely prepared for a sophisticated parody of symbolism.

The last of this group of works is the story, "Ex Centro," published in 1911 in *Večery* (literary supplement to *Lidové noviny*). One wonders why this tale was never republished by the brothers, since it is one of the most interesting of their early narratives.[3] Two sophisticates sitting in a box at the *variété* talk about love, exchanging epigrams on woman and her frailty. Finally one confesses that he dreams of loving a female puppet, for a puppet can never possess the eternal contradiction of woman; it can never hate or deceive. In the performance which follows a brother and sister appear on the flying trapeze. Intoxicated by the success of his wild performance, the acrobat whirls the girl about the bar ever more rapidly until he kills her, then throws her down on the stage as a child throws down a broken doll, screeching the single word, "Poupée!" From a box there comes the answering cry of "puppet!" After the performance it is not only the acrobat who is driven off to the madhouse, but the sophisticate as well. In the asylum he ends his days peacefully, content to play with a large puppet which he introduces to everyone as his mistress.

Here again (though for the last time in the brothers' work) the image of woman as puppet appears. The puppet was, of course, a traditional image of the symbolists, who used it to suggest man's impotence in the hands of fate or his lack of real individuality. But the Čapeks apply it only to woman: in "L'Éventail" it symbolizes her enigmatic contradictions; in "Ex Centro" her ideal compliance. Love is, for the young Čapeks, a puppet comedy, in which man only becomes more and more deeply involved in the web of contradictions of human nature, which can be eliminated only at the cost of human individuality. In *R.U.R.*, Karel was to investigate the tempting possibility that man can achieve utopia by the same sacrifice of individuality. But the price of such a sacrifice, of course, are life and love themselves. The puppet is a symbol of a dream of eliminating the endless contradictions which are within man. But these contradictions are life itself, and can be resolved only in a grotesque imitation of man which is spiritually dead.[4]

Thus the brothers' first period came to an end. Though their writing still remained subjectivist and impressionistic, they already reacted violently against the decadent strain in symbolism. They attempted new forms in the impressionistic journalism of the Vienna school and the neo-classical tale of Ernst. Both these forms proved too limited for further development.

5. The Luminous Depths

The neo-classical period had been only a passing phase in the work of the Brothers Čapek, though the formal discipline it provided is felt in several new stories they published in 1911 and 1912. These, along with the two Italian tales, were subsequently collected in the volume published in 1916 as *The Luminous Depths*.[1] Vitalism is the main force animating these tales, and the cynicism of the earlier pieces has disappeared almost completely. But the new faith in life brings a fresh skepticism: granting that life is self-valuable, is man capable of comprehending its innate worth? Will human civilization not frustrate natural life? Thus the whole collection turns in a circle leading the authors from cynical irony through optimism, and back to pessimism.

The story "A Scandal and the Press" is a new experiment in the technique of narrative fiction. Though not published until 1916 in the collected edition of *The Luminous Depths*, the story was probably written in 1911, during the brothers' stay in Paris or soon thereafter. It is likely that Karel Čapek was its chief, if not its sole, author.[2] The subject is a scandal which occurred in Paris in 1911, when an aristocrat feigned suicide to run off to Canada with the governess of his children.[3] Čapek has made a concise, dry summary of the newspaper accounts without changing the names, and adding only a few brief comments on the techniques of modern criminology and journalism.

The story appears to be an attempt to introduce the technique of reporting into narrative fiction. But in fact it is not reporting, of course, for Čapek is not the first reporter of the events he recounts, but only an ironic treatment of reporting. The real story is, in spite of considerable suspense and a surprise ending, rare in real life, a dull and trivial affair. This is presumably the ironic point of Čapek's treatment: the story is banal, and only sensational methods of the press have succeeded in making a scandal of it. But the irony is too slight. The topical quality of the story hardly accords with the other tales of the collection, which are set either in an exotic past, or in no prescribed period or place. The most interesting element of the story, perhaps, is one which is only slightly implicit: an anticipation of Čapek's later relativism. Not only are people not what they seem (M. d'Abbadie d'Arrast was a devout Catholic and exemplary husband), but the newspaper account created to satisfy the public taste for scandal is not the real truth either. Last of all, the story is a first instance of Čapek's fascination with narratives of crime and detection.

The next two stories in the collection are exclusively Karel's work, and were originally published in periodicals over his signature. The first of these, "Between Two Kisses," is the tale of a man whose whole life is a sacrifice to personal egoism. Only too late does he realize that the two kisses which framed the long interval of his life were the only thing of value in it. In its praise of life and love, the story seems optimistic, of course. But there is another, perhaps unconscious, implication: man is incapable of finding his happiness, and will recognize it only when it is too late.[4]

"The Island"[5] is the story of a Portuguese nobleman who is shipwrecked on an exotic island and lives with a tribe of savages. Taking a native mistress, he sinks into indolence, forgets his own language, and neglects to learn hers. One day a Portuguese ship lands on the island. Making himself known to the ship's officers in broken syllables, the shipwrecked man begs them to take him home. They remind him of the joys of his homeland and his native speech, in which he can again "converse, relate his adventures and pour out his feelings," for "there is nothing more beautiful" than the human power of speech. But then he remembers his native mistress, her love for him, and her solicitude for his comfort. Unable to leave her,

he conceals himself until the ship sails away. The rest of his life he
never speaks again.

The point of the story is that language, noble as it is, is not life.
Life is feeling and love; language is only a part of that civilization
which stands in contradiction to life. Language is a communal instrument which cancels out the intangible differences between
human beings, though these differences constitute man's individuality—that which is most important to him. In spite of all the precision of language in naming objects about us, it is a feeble instrument when used to describe the world of emotion and spirit within.
Čapek was apparently led to this rather artificial opposition of
language and life by his study of Bergson and the pragmatists. He
exalts the intuitive, the indefinable, the irrational and individual,
over that which is conventional, rational and communal.

The final tale of the volume is the title story, "The Luminous
Depths," the joint work of the two brothers. It is fairly easy to
guess the contribution of each: to Josef probably belongs the strong
lyrical element in the story, while the philosophic and analytical
strain is almost undoubtedly Karel's. The story's subject, or rather,
its point of departure, is the sinking of the liner *Titanic*, for the
purposes of fiction renamed the *Oceanic*.

A passenger on the liner several times observes a beautiful young
girl whom he longs to meet. When the ship strikes an iceberg, he
sees her again for a fleeting moment, but then she is lost to him
forever. He is rescued, but she perishes, and he cannot even learn her
name. His life seems to him to lose all value, to become "an illusion,
which will end in nothing." The girl is clearly a symbol, standing in
a sense for both life and death: she appears to him for an instant at
the moment when he thinks he will die; but, deprived of her, he feels
himself spiritually dead. Thus the authors suggest those "luminous
depths" of the subconscious in which love, which is life, passes over
into the wish for death.

In the middle of the lyricized narrative a piece of philosophical
ratiocination is inserted: man's creation becomes ever more perfect,
but the perfection of his technology only serves to hurl him more
swiftly toward the doom which fate sets in his way:

Endlessly man's works become more perfect and more efficient; ever they approach human reason itself and come to resemble it more closely. But from their beginning they appear in *two series:* one, in which man's constructive creativity, with all its great achievements, goes forward according to the laws of causality and order; the other, a series of imperfections, lawless and uncaused, generated by disorder, unconquerable and therefore eternally indomitable to man, for this is the series of the unconscious and of chaos. Life moves continually through both series; the extension of one series involves the extension of the other, and ever-new perfection brings new possibilities for imperfection... But even this rule of destruction is no law; if it were a *law*, man could master it, but he will never do so.

This pessimistic conclusion does not, of course, directly contradict the earlier vitalist philosophy, for what is under discussion here is human civilization, and not the inner life of the spirit. But the point is that man's spirit is at the mercy of his civilization, his own creation. History is seen as irrational, beyond the domain of natural law. There can be no escape, for the destructive energy of civilization may destroy us as well. Thus the story is a link between "The System" and *R.U.R.*; man's works are the death of the spirit unless they are animated by spirit and life themselves. For Karel Čapek only *individual* creation is free from suspicion. The creativity of the artist is good, for it shapes an organic thing, something of life itself. That of the worker is good, for it supports life. But the creations of the technologist or even of the statesman only ease life; they neither embody life nor sustain it.

"The Luminous Depths" is a first attempt by the brothers at a kind of "literary cubism." The Czech critic Miroslav Rutte describes the new style thus:

Literary cubism lays bare the event and breaks down phenomena into fine planes so that it can reveal the mechanism of fate and the order of occurrences, so that by the analysis of concrete forms it can penetrate to the essences, in space and time, of metaphysical forms. It analyzes consciously so that it can reach the subconscious. It arranges, classifies and calculates so that it can measure that which is concealed.[6]

To be sure, this "cubism" is something of a trick; the effect of analysis of different "planes" is achieved in "The Luminous Depths" largely by the mechanical combination of lyrical and philosophical styles, and from this point of view the story is a failure. In his next collection Čapek was to perfect this union of lyricism and philosophical analysis.

6. The Lost Way

In 1917 Čapek published a collection of metaphysical tales, *Wayside Crosses*. Never very popular, and for the most part not translated into English,[1] these stories none the less belong to his finest and most serious work.

Wayside Crosses reflects a deep pessimism, partly due to the war, partly to a spiritual crisis in Čapek's life. Dissatisfied with his earlier, superficial vitalism, and uncertain of the optimistic teachings of Bergson and the pragmatists, Čapek undertakes in this collection an agonized search for absolute spiritual values. Again and again the quest ends in failure, not because the absolute Čapek seeks does not exist, but because man, imprisoned in the relative world of his own being, cannot find it. Man can conceive of Absolute God, but he cannot comprehend Him or communicate with Him. Nor can God communicate with man, for He too is a prisoner of His own absolute being. *Wayside Crosses* is infused with a mood of nostalgic regret at the failure of the search for God.

In 1928 Čapek replied to a student group which had questioned him concerning his religious beliefs: he declared that he differed from Masaryk in not being of "religious dispositon. I have not gone so far; for the time being I am content with faith in the possibility of belief." And, asked if his earlier collection of religious tales was not the result of a conversion experience, he replied:

A conversion in *Wayside Crosses?* I doubt it. The actual theme of *Wayside Crosses* is partly the war (and waiting for the miracle that it would turn out well for us), and partly—on the basis of a mistaken diagnosis—a supposedly fatal illness and thus a kind of reckoning with life. In a sense it is a conversion: not to faith, however, but to sympathy... The name *Wayside Crosses* is ambiguous, and means, on one hand, a parting of the ways; on the other, self-torment with the things of the highest and with searching.[2]

The medical opinion Čapek refers to here is undoubtedly the motive force behind the spiritual crisis we sense in the book; otherwise we know nothing of that crisis. But it cannot be said that *Wayside Crosses* represents a surrender to God from fear; the book is an agonized record of the search for God, but God ultimately eludes the pursuer, who comes through the crisis with sympathy for man rather than faith in God.

Earlier Čapek had said of the book that "*Wayside Crosses* signifies that the search for truth is more than truth itself... If each act of comprehension is limited, [still] the road to truth itself is spiritually unlimited."[3]

The name contains a multiple ambiguity which is significant. *Boží muka* means literally, "God's torment," i.e., Calvary. In popular speech the phrase is used to denote crucifixes and wayside shrines. A wayside shrine is a place of religious awe, miracle, and legend; at the same time, located at a crossroads, it is a symbol of decision or of parting. But the phrase also retains something of its original meaning: "God's torment"—for God cannot reach out to man; also "man's torment because of God," for man's search for the divine ends in failure.

Like Chesterton, Čapek uses the detective story form as an allegory of the search for God: Chesterton's novel, *The Man Who Was Thursday*, was the specific model. But Čapek is better aware than Chesterton that God's existence may only be intuited; it cannot be deduced. "God cannot be found by the technique of criminal investigation," Holeček says in the story called "Elegy." The use of the detective story form underlines the ineffectiveness of the detective's methods. Čapek later wrote, "I once attempted to write a volume of detective stories...; out of it finally came *Wayside Crosses*. No one, alas, saw detective stories in that collection. Evidently I did not quite succeed."[4] This is modesty, no doubt, for the form of the detective story has been distorted deliberately to fit the metaphysical content. As Mukařovský points out, the narrative itself is suppressed; there is only a detective situation.[5] Thus Čapek achieves at least a part of the suspense of the detective's quest, but at the same time deliberately foregoes the solution, which cannot be given, for here the quest never attains its goal.

A number of the stories of the collection describe miracles, for the miracle is a manifestation of the Absolute's existence. But Čapek is not really concerned whether or not miracles may occur. He seems to assume that they can, at least in the lives of some persons. His skepticism is directed rather to the question: what use are miracles to man? They indeed remind us that God exists. But we cannot comprehend or accept them, for they are mysteries, as God Himself is. Our minds instinctively reject them. We need them for our salvation, but if they occur we cannot use them, for they cannot affect us in the world of relative and rationalistic values.

This is the subject of three tales, "The Footprint," "Elegy," and "Reflections." In the first tale two men find a mysterious, single footprint in the fresh snow. There are no other tracks near it in the empty field. Hume's speculations concerning an isolated print in the sand are the obvious source of the theme, and Boura, the professional philosopher of the tale, refers to them. He can explain the footprint only as a miracle. But it is a miracle which is impotent. Would a more "useful" miracle be more effective? The two men are inclined to doubt it:

"If someone here were to resurrect a dead girl, you would kneel down and humble yourself, but before the snow would have melted from your knees, the thought would occur to you that she only seemed to be dead."... "Perhaps I would not believe even in that resurrection. But I too want to be saved and I wait for a miracle—for something to come and change my life. That footprint will not change me and will not save me, and will redeem me from nothing; it only torments me, it obsesses me and I cannot get rid of it. And I do not believe it; a miracle would content me, but that footprint is the first step to uncertainty. It would be better if I had not seen it."

Divine miracles have nothing to do with man, for, coming from the Absolute, they are incomprehensible to man.

In "Elegy; the Footprint II," the two men meet again and recall
their miraculous experience. In a wine cellar they find Boura's elder
brother, who had disappeared many years before. The two brothers
recall their common past, but it is obvious that they have little to
say: the real truth cannot be communicated. Forgetting his walking
stick, the elder brother starts to leave. Holeček runs out to give it
to him, but finds the entrance and the street empty. Two policemen
coming in testify that they have not passed him; nor can he be
found in the cellar. Boura is not surprised at the happening, for his
brother kept disappearing in this way all his life. Uneducated, he
has no conception of the limits of natural law. Again there is a
miracle, and again it is useless. But perhaps not quite useless, as
Boura observes:

"In us too there are such events and happenings, which perhaps have
no other purpose than their own perfection. Sudden moments of freedom—even if they are only moments. If things happened in a way
natural for our souls, *miracles would occur.*"

In "Reflections" a sick man who spends his days gazing at the water
fancies he sees God in the chance ripplings which he observes:

"That happens very rarely. And then I think: why couldn't it be God?
Perhaps He is just that which is most fleeting in the world; perhaps His
reality is a sudden breaking of a wave and a flash; it happens incom-
prehensibly, as an exception, and then it passes. It is possible that in
people too there occurs just such a rippling or a flash, and again it breaks.
It must break. True reality must be paid for by destruction."

Miracles are possible, then, but true miracles occur *within* man.
And hence they are indemonstrable. Man cannot believe in them,
for he lives chiefly in the world of natural law. Only a sudden flash
of intuition can bring him close to God. If miracle is the only way
in which God can communicate with man, intuition is man's only
path to God. What Čapek is describing in these tales is not the reality
of miracles as such, but the type of cognition which is capable of
perceiving them. Reason can never do this. As Boura says later in
"Elegy" of his experience of the footprint, "How close was that
footprint to me then! But later, from the standpoint of truth, I began to hate it."

Moments of intuition such as this are the subjects of "Elegy" and of two more tales, "The Lost Way" and "The Motto." Čapek's distrust of reason and his faith in intuition derive from Bergson and the pragmatists. In "Elegy" Boura comes to the conclusion that "truth does not matter," that "there is something more than truth, which does not bind, but liberates." This "something more" is never defined, but it is apparent that Čapek is here opposing a rationalistic truth to the broader conception of pragmatic "truth"— personal, sometimes intuitive, flexible according to the needs of the individual. Still, his faith in pragmatism seems equivocal. If man knows truth only in brief intuitive flashes, how can it serve him? For the greater part of his life he is in bondage to reason, which only dispels his flashes of deeper insight.

This intuitive "truth" cannot be analyzed or communicated, and most often it cannot even be believed. It is fleeting, and man has little more than a sense of its existence. This is the point of the tale, "The Lost Way." Two men walking in the dark lose their way and stumble into an open field. There one of them suddenly grasps the truth of his whole existence, of how he ought to live. But when they come back onto the road, he loses the new insight forever. The road obviously symbolizes a form limiting thought, which man must nevertheless accept as a condition of thought. Man's thought is relative; absolute truth "exists," but not for man: it resembles a field of two dimensions, while the road man follows has only one, as one of the characters observes:

"Truth must be experienced before it can become a word. You must find yourself in it as in a space which leads nowhere, but opens on all sides, for your thought is only a road going in one direction, like a passageway between walls. Your thought goes only forward on one of many roads, but truth, which is single, goes nowhere and is headed nowhere, but stands like an open space."

Here we see that Čapek's conception is quite different from pragmatism; indeed, his position is reversed. That "thought" which "goes forward on one of many roads" is relativistic thought, which serves the purpose of the individual, which takes him along whatever road he wishes to follow. This "thought" is pragmatic truth. But this "truth" Čapek sees as a prisoner of the very road it has chosen. Beside it there is a higher, absolute truth which "goes nowhere and is headed nowhere." But, though man senses the existence of this truth, he cannot comprehend it, for, "like an open space," it will not conform to the necessary conditions of thought and language. At the end of the story the insight of the open field is forgetten completely.

The same conclusion is reached in "The Motto." A sick man discovers, scrawled on the wall at the head of his bed, the words, "Go back" *(nazpět)*. Evidently he had written this many years before, but he cannot remember when or why. In vain he tries to guess the meaning. The motto is apparently a reminder of an insight he once had, but failed to act upon. Now he realizes that there is no return in time, and that the insight is gone forever.

Čapek's preoccupation with illness in these tales is personal, of course. But it is also a testimony to his discovery that illness may sharpen our powers of intuition by freeing us from the pressures of practical life. Like William James, he was aware of the possibility that truth may come to us in abnormal states more readily than in normal ones.

But cannot man compel the Absolute, force it to yield to his insistence? Must man be content with passive waiting for a miracle?

This is the theme of "The Mountain," the longest and in some respects the best of these tales. A body is found that has evidently been pushed from a cliff. There is no identification, for the murderer has removed all identification from the dead man's clothing. The murderer is a stranger in the district. He tries to flee, but cannot escape. The police drive him farther and farther from civilization. Finally he climbs to the top of a mountain. Everyone who sees him fears him, for he is a stranger, huge, frightening, with a powerful voice. No one sees his face, which is always covered. The irrational terror he inspires drives his pursuers to the conclusion that he is someone not of their world, that his deed has taken him outside the real world and into the irrational one of the Absolute. They surround the mountain in an early morning fog and advance toward the top. He eludes them, however, and only one of them succeeds in talking with him in the fog. He finds that the murderer, far from being terrible, is weak and pitiful: he calls again and again on God to save him, and refuses the help which the other seeks to give him. In the end he kills himself, jumping from a cliff, just as he had pushed his victim from one. His identity and mystery are never revealed.

The story seems most intelligible in the light of the metaphysical significance given the criminal act by Dostoevski or the existentialists. Crime is an attempt by the individual to pass outside the bonds of human society, to come face-to-face with the essence of irrational spirit; to discover whether divine spirit exists, or if the only spirit is within oneself, in which case man is himself the Absolute. Raskolnikov kills the old pawnbroker women in *Crime and Punishment* in an attempt to make himself God; in the irrational act of self-assertion he hopes to discover the Absolute within himself. But in the end he finds it without; he has indeed put himself outside the world of human society, but only to come face to face with divine law. There can be no doubt that Čapek, who venerated Dostoevski above all other novelists,[6] is following Dostoevski here. His treatment is most unlike Dostoevski, however, and rather resembles Chesterton. The formal use of the detective story as an allegory of man's search for God suggests *The Man Who Was Thursday*, of course. There is at least one striking parallel between Chesterton's novel and "The Mountain": the tremendous size of the unknown murderer and the irrational fear he inspires. Chesterton's Sunday turns out to be God; in Čapek's tale, men are haunted by the dread that he may be God. But they are mistaken, and this distinction serves to underline Čapek's originality. In Dostoevski the rebellion against God is essentially ethical, and Raskolnikov finds God because he has sinned. In Čapek's tale the attack is metaphysical: the murderer reminds man of God because both murder and God have in common the element of irrational mystery. Both are outside human society, and incomprehensible. Čapek is concerned with metaphysics rather than ethics: in the party which hunts down the murderer in his tale there is no saint or priest; there is a police chief and his subordinates, and two laymen—a metaphysician and a composer.

The assault upon the Absolute fails. The murderer puts himself beyond society, and it drives him to the mountain and over the cliff. At the summit, the traditional place of meeting with God, the murderer finds no Absolute; only terror and weakness within himself. He, too, has confused his irrational act with God. God does not

reveal Himself, though the murderer calls on Him pitifully. Cast out
by man and unable to find God, he must destroy himself. Here
again the ending suggests Dostoevski: in the first plan for *Crime and
Punishment*, Raskolnikov was to commit suicide. But Dostoevski
wanted to believe in the redemptive power of divine love; Čapek,
the metaphysician, doubts: for him the moment of mystical truth
must inevitably pass and be lost. There can be no meeting with God
on the mountain, for the Absolute will not be compelled.

In this tale Čapek is concerned as much with the pursuers as the
pursued. How does the man who lives rationally in society react
when confronted with the irrational mystery of the Absolute? And
here Čapek gives us the first of his relativist studies of a variety of
points of view, reflecting the variety of personality in man himself.
The story reminds us of his later novel, *Meteor* (1934), and indeed we
find striking parallels. In both narratives a number of people try to
fathom the life of a mysterious stranger, and each reacts differently
to the mystery: it is himself whom he attempts to substitute for the
mystery, and each solution is therefore different.

Only the composer Jevíšek is able to comprehend the mystery of
the unknown man, but he can comprehend it solely in his art, and
his discovery can be communicated only as art. It is he who discovers that the unknown man is weak and pitiful, and that he has
much in common with each of his pursuers. This discovery brings us
back to Čapek's statement that in *Wayside Crosses* there is a conversion, "not to faith... but to sympathy." Only here does Čapek
pass from metaphysics to ethics: the awful mystery of the Absolute
is a reminder that man is a prisoner of his own being, that he
torments himself in his quest for God, and hence he is pitiful. Čapek
discovers not God but man in *Wayside Crosses*.

The metaphysician Slavík wants an answer to mystery, and hence
he joins in the chase. But in the end he gives up his quest as hopeless: we cannot know the truth of God, or even of another man's
life. We can only feel a sense of mystery.

The police chief is the man of action, confronted by an irrational
act which disrupts society. Not reason is the answer, he knows,
but reassertion of order. His dialogue with Slavík is instructive:

"Yes," objected Slavík, "but instead of solving a mystery, we are only trying to investigate it. To conduct an official hearing, simply. That's just what I don't like. It's terribly unsophisticated. Perhaps we will catch him, but then we will have only the crude interest of the fact itself. Mystery is a matter for the soul, each riddle is pervaded by the breath of the spirit, as it were. Only when he meets a mystery, does man become conscious of his own spirit, and he feels trembling and fear. *Timor Dei...* The fear of the spirit. Materialism is quite without mystery. Without fear. Without the courage for fear. In a word, I wanted a solution which would be more internal..."

"You wanted a more internal solution?" the police chief echoed suddenly. "But in professional work there are no internal solutions. Perhaps it would be possible to make a field fertile simply by praying, but it would be bad technically. Perhaps internal methods are the shortest and most direct of all, but they are technically incorrect. Perhaps it would be possible to solve a crime by simple moral intuition, but intuition is unspecialized. All detectives in novels work badly in a technical sense. Too personally, too inventively. Their methods are those of a criminal and not a detective's. The real way is different."

"What?"

"Social routine. Organization. Look, there exists a technique for mastering people—a real technique, because it deals with man as with an instrument. There is progress in that; what was once a personal art, is now becoming a technique. Everything we touch turns into an instrument. Even man. Even yourself. Only the *one up above* escapes us."

"God?"

"No, man.[7] The criminal who flees."

At the end of the story Jevíšek discovers that all of them have something in common with the man on the mountain: all of them fear and are tormented in the search for God, and hence all of them are pitiful:

He saw Slavík torturing himself with the sorrow of self-reproach and self-torment; he saw how tired the chief was, how exhausted; he was bowed over by the grief and weakness of a sick child. "You could all understand him," he felt, "all of you! He was so unhappy, and he was only trying to escape—how well you could understand him!"

The story is the first successful example of Čapek's new technique of "literary cubism." The narrative is fragmented into a number of short episodes which portray the different characters and their separate flashes of insight. Their reactions to the mystery correspond to the different planes or viewpoints represented in a cubist painting. We may better call this technique that of perspectivism: the construction of a cumulative series of viewpoints each of which contributes something to the entire picture. Perspectivism goes beyond relativism; perspectivism is a cooperative union of various viewpoints to create truth; relativism is simply the skeptical assertion that various viewpoints are possible.[8] In this respect Čapek is far in advance of the relativism of Pirandello's play *Così è, se vi pare* (1917; English translation as "Right You Are If You Think You Are"), for example. He is even ahead of his own relativism of the 1920s, in which he simply gives various viewpoints which are contradictory but which do not contribute to any composite truth. Here again "The Mountain" reminds us of *Meteor*.

The failure of the search for God leads us back to man and to sympathy for him. This theme is most forcibly expressed in the closing story of the collection, "Help!" A man is wakened by a woman's cry for help. But no one is there when he goes to the door, and the cry is never repeated. He reflects that he has waited his whole life for such a cry, for a command from God, a miracle to redeem him: "for a great event to happen, a sudden light pouring through the chinks, for the sound of heavy blows on the door and a powerful voice commanding, 'Lazarus, arise!'... Perhaps it would not be a voice of command, but one begging for help, 'Lazarus, arise that you may help us!'"

But Čapek is not yet certain whether man deserves help. Is not man too dehumanized by society and civilization to deserve the miracle of our sympathy, to accept it and use it? His distrust of the individual, formerly symbolized in the image of the puppet, returns.

Two stories, "Lída" and "Love Song—Lída II," are concerned with this doubt. In the first story a young girl disappears. Her family fears that she is dead, but the friend to whom they appeal for help is convinced that she has run off with a lover. Her actions are typical and statistically predictable, he concludes sadly, and decides that he can find her by a combination of deductive reasoning and intuition. He succeeds all too easily: in fact Lída has run off with a worthless man who soon deserts her.

The story reminds us of the early feuilleton, "The Unit," from

The Garden of Krakonoš. Society is not concerned with our individuality, which it neither notices nor respects, but only with our conformity to rules and statistics. Our behavior is predictable and determined. Free will seemingly does not exist. Where then is man's individuality?

The question is answered in "Love Song (Lída II)," though not directly. Lída returns home, crushed and self-tormented. Holub, the "detective," comes to visit her and hopes for a miracle which will restore her self-confidence and trust in life. And his hope is finally rewarded: Lída falls in love with him. Love, then, is the answer: in love man is free and in love he can transcend himself.

Wayside Crosses also contains a number of mood pictures, several of which are concerned with the theme of waiting. "Time Stands Still" is a literal attempt to imitate a cubist painting in a word picture: to describe a frozen moment of inner suffering in absolute silence, to depict it as an eternal essence, motionless and unchanging until time reasserts its existence in the sound of the steps of a by-passer.

"The Waiting Room" is a dialogue conducted by two men who spend the night waiting in a railway station. Waiting is life itself, yet it is the hardest thing in life. We wait for redemption, and whatever comes to end our waiting is a redemption. At the end of the tale, day breaks and the long night's wait is ended. The story reflects the mood of the war, as does "Help!," which also ends with the dawn of a new day.

Thus Čapek emerged from the self-torment of *Wayside Crosses*, without belief in God, but with the expectation of redemption, without faith in man, but with sympathy for him. This sympathy for man was to concern him in his next collection.

7. The Offended

Between 1918 and 1920 Čapek published a number of short stories, subsequently collected under the title of *Painful Tales* (1921).[1] Unlike *Wayside Crosses*, these are tales of everyday life, realistic in tone. With their melancholy mood, coming from introspective reminiscence, and with the *pointe* of the tale usually blunted, they recall the stories of Chekhov. The situations are more ironic than is customary in Chekhov, however, and may well remind the reader rather of Maupassant.

Each of the stories depicts a character caught in a life dilemma which he is unable to resolve. The conflict is one involving a choice between two levels of good, or of evil, and it is this conflict of moral interest which becomes so painful.

Critics have considered *Painful Tales* as Čapek's most pessimistic work. František Götz supposes that its pessimism stems from the failure of the search for God in *Wayside Crosses*.[2] But this interpretation is founded on a miscomprehension of the earlier volume. The search for God had failed, but it led in turn to the discovery of sympathy for man. It is this new-found sympathy with which Čapek turns to man in *Painful Tales*. True, in a sense Götz is right: just as man torments himself in the search for God, so he torments himself in the urge to do good beyond his powers. Man cannot achieve absolute good any more than he can find Absolute God, for he is imprisoned in a world of relative values. Hence he is faced constantly by situations in which one good conflicts with another. And his intuitive sense that there is absolute justice makes it impossible for him to choose. Even if he acts selfishly or in a cowardly manner, deeper insight may show that he is trying to achieve justice.

This relativity of values is accompanied by a relativity of viewpoints. The story is presented to the reader so that his interpretation of events will be contradictory, so that he too is left without basis for choice. As Mukařovský says, there is a conflict between an "external," superficial evaluation of the facts of the story, and an inner one, only partly revealed, that of the characters themselves. Mukařovský presents several examples of this contradiction:

External View	*Internal View*
A faithless wife and a husband who exploits her faithlessness, but at the same time...	two people driven by fate and full of mutual sympathy. *("Three")*
A lonely petty official, who refuses to help his sisters in need, but at the same time...	a sensitive man, who longs to sacrifice himself for others and is wounded by the greed of those about him. *("Money")*
A widower and official, angered at the dishonesty of his housekeeper..., whom he catches stealing from him, but at the same time...	an old and weak man, afraid of being left alone. *("The Shirts")*[3]

Such contradictions are not new in literature, of course, but for Čapek they are not incidental ironies; they are rooted in the essence of human action. Čapek himself said of the stories:

Painful Tales return to the theme: each man has his own truth. For here people act badly, cowardly, cruelly, or weakly, in a word, painfully, and the whole point is that you cannot condemn any of them... I wanted to show man in humiliation and weakness, without debasing his value as a human being.[4]

In "Three," a husband forces his wife to beg from her lover, first some cloth for an overcoat, then money. Still he loves her, and is deeply unhappy.

"Helena" begins as an idyll, with the meeting of a mature man and a sensitive girl. Their friendship is a warm one, but she is awkward and naive, and he cannot love her. She mistakes their intimacy for love, and sends him an ardent letter. Before he can answer, she comes to see him. Embarrassed, he tells her he is too old to believe in love. Though he tries to be considerate, he feels that his rejection is an act of brutality, and so she interprets it.

"At the Castle" describes the life of a governess on a country estate. The count treats her well, but refuses to believe that his little daughter, her pupil, is rude and stupid. The countess suspects the governess of stealing and searches her room. The English tutor torments her with his frank sexuality and his impudent advances. Though she dines with the count's family, the maids regard her as a servant. She determines to give up her place. But a letter arrives from home describing her family's pathetic circumstances, and she realizes that for others her life is only enviable. The story recalls Čapek's own stay on the estate of Count Vladimír Lažanský in 1916–1917, but there is nothing in it which is demonstrably autobiographical.

"Money" is the tale of a man who loves his two sisters and is willing to sacrifice himself to help them. But he cannot endure their hatred of one another, their envy, their lies and bickering, and in the end he turns his back on both of them.

In "The Brute," a wife wishes to leave her wealthy husband for the man she loves. The husband is certain that she cannot forego the luxury to which his money has accustomed her. But he ignores the possibility that love could change her. In the end he drives the two apart.

"The Shirts" is the story of a widower who suspects that his housekeeper has been stealing from him. He searches her cupboards and finds many of his personal possessions. When he confronts her with the evidence, she only takes offense at his invasion of her privacy. He begs her to stay on, but she leaves, her pride wounded. He realizes sadly that now he is left completely alone.

"The Offended Man" tells of an official who is unjustly insulted by a superior for a supposed error. He spends the night with a prostitute. In the morning he goes to his brother's and asks him to inform his wife that he will not return to her, and that he does not love her. Only little by little does the actual story come out. The brother obtains an official apology for the misunderstanding, and tells the wife that her husband is coming home.

"The Tribunal" is the only story in the book which departs from realism. A military judge has justly condemned a soldier for killing and robbing a wounded comrade. Suddenly he hears an inner voice telling him that there is neither law nor justice, neither conscience nor God. He realizes that his action was in fact arbitrary and tyrannical. His cloak of justice and authority is stripped off, and he is left weak and pitiful. In this story Čapek carries his conviction that there are no absolutes to its extreme: to the philosophy of "If there is no God, then all is lawful," as one of Dostoevski's characters expresses it. And this is the logical conclusion of *Painful Tales* as a whole: they are a record of the weakness of man lost in a world where there is only conflict between values.

This conflict and the quality of sympathy the author extends to his suffering heroes are the best things in *Painful Tales*. Čapek found no new approach with which to revitalize the realistic short story. Neither in style nor character portrayal are these tales new; Čapek had not yet mastered the technique of deft, economical characterization through turns of speech, so marked in his later work: in the "Tales from Two Pockets" (1929), or in *Hordubal* (1933), for example. But he has chosen subjects entirely appropriate to his theme, and has sustained the mood of self-doubt and self-torment which he sought.

8. The Outlaw

Čapek's first full-length play, *The Outlaw*, had its première at the National Theater in Prague on March 2, 1920.[1] Eva Vrchlická, the daughter of the poet Vrchlický and a leading actress, played the role of Mimi.

The Outlaw is a comedy of youth and love. Here are the joy and the pain of youth, its struggle for self-awareness, its conflict with the entrenched power of age, the ecstasy and fleetingness of love. It is a comedy with strong overtones of melodrama and tragedy. But Čapek has kept the comic note dominant, and even broadened it at times to farce. He has this to say concerning the origin of the play:

> The conception and the first version of this play came in Paris in 1911. It was born of homesickness, of the difficulty of coming to terms with Paris, and of the sharp ache of life abroad; it grew with the remembrance of youth and freedom, of my birthplace and comrades, of my homeland. It was not only a remembrance, however, but a leavetaking.
>
> Friends of those days, witness for the author if his *Outlaw* is not at least a little a portrayal of you. You, who danced at the Zátiší, made a grab at every girl, picked every rose, and at the same time raised the flag of revolt against prevailing taste in art... What joy and what pride is there in the feeling that we are the younger generation!... But when the author came back to you with his first version in his pocket, he saw that you too had taken leave of that youth. *The Outlaw* remained a torso which lacked an ending.
>
> Twice later the author returned to *The Outlaw*, the first time to change him into an American pioneer, full of energy as a Leyden jar. The second

time he turned him into a symbolic personage, a god of youth with all the miraculous signs of primitive divinity. Fortunately both plans came to naught. During the war the author's nostalgia for the idea of leave-taking returned to him, but he was stopped by the complete improbability of a play about the outlaw at a time when that great robust fellow must have been a soldier.

And so only now after eight years has the author attempted a reconstruction of his original plan, changing as little as possible of its quality of youth; only the outlaw himself, who was then twenty, has now attained thirty.[2]

It is difficult to relate *The Outlaw* to any of the works discussed so far. In style it is quite distinct, with its fresh and often comical use of popular and dialect speech. The impulse to write a play of love and youth can easily be related to Čapek's youth and the sojourn in Paris, but the treatment of love is strikingly different from anything he published at that time. Gone is the early ironic attitude toward love, the endless circle of the lover's doubt, the mechanical triviality of the process of falling in and out of love. In conception the play is closer to "Love Song" in *Wayside Crosses* (1917), than to the early pieces.

The mixture of realist and symbolist styles in *The Outlaw* also suggests a later time of composition. The theme of love frustrated by parental intervention is reminiscent of the subjects of *Painful Tales*. The strong note of relativism in the play also recalls that collection. Nor is there in the text of *The Outlaw* as we have it any of that specific quality of nostalgia for his homeland which Čapek speaks of. Hence it seems probable that the final version is largely the work of the postwar years. Čapek's statement does not contradict this: he speaks of "a reconstruction of his original plan, changing as little as possible of its *quality of youth*." What he means, apparently, is that the freshness and spontaneity of his original conception of young love has been preserved. He says nothing about situation, plot, or treatment of character.

The outlaw himself is a nihilist, brazen, self-reliant, a fearless champion of the rights of young love. His appellative (he has no name) is a symbol of his self-assertion: he steals even love from the prison fashioned for it by the older generation. He is in fact that symbolic "god of youth" of Čapek's earlier conception.

In his wanderings the outlaw chances upon a young girl, Mimi, whose father, a pedantic professor, keeps constant guard over her. Her elder sister had escaped to run off with a man who soon deserted her. The father has built a veritable fortress in the country to hold his younger daughter prisoner. Called away for a day, the parents go with apprehension, leaving Mimi in the care of the servant Fanka, a virago as vigilant and strict as they. But the outlaw contrives to speak with Mimi. Intuitively he guesses her hard lot. Awakened by his sympathy, she falls deeply in love.

The hero then sets himself the task of driving off her rival suitor, a forester. Brazenly he insults the other, drives him to a fury, and challenges him to shoot. In a panic, the forester fires, and the outlaw is wounded. Carried off to the village, he promises Mimi to return.

The same night he comes back. Fanka is asleep, and Mimi steals down to meet him. In this love scene the dialogue passes from prose to verse. The transition is awkward, but there is a gain in expressiveness. In any case, the change is as much one in lexicon and style (which inevitably change in a love scene) as in prosodic form, for the iambic verses of irregular lengths, mostly unrhymed, can be read almost as prose. There is occasional rhyme, however, as well as assonance, which is more disturbing. It is possible that this scene in verse is a remnant of the original Paris version. The lovers' dialogue is interrupted by the unexpected return of the parents, who have had a premonition of evil.

Driven off again, the outlaw returns early the next morning. Mimi has sworn to her parents that she will not speak to him, but the moment she sees him she breaks her promise. The professor, his wife, and Fanka come out to drive him away, but he deftly steals into the house and locks it, turning their own fortress against them. Appearing on the balcony with a gun, he announces his intention of fighting for Mimi's right to choose. He will repel any attack. The professor sends for the local authorities. These are comic figures who have spent the preceding evening drinking with the outlaw in the local inn, and they derive immense enjoyment from the situation. Finally sobered by the professor's threats, they beg the young man to leave, but he will not listen. They refuse to take further steps, and the professor sends Fanka for the state police. Now the personal drama of the parents unfolds. They reveal that when they were young they waited eight years for one another, eight years of toil and self-denial. For the professor this is the essence of love, but his wife regrets that they were not bolder. They were sensible, but love has eluded them. The professor curses the bandit who has taken everything he possessed in life: his house, his daughter, even his sense that he loves and is loved.

Meanwhile the elder sister returns, veiled; she has learned of Mimi's love affair, and comes to warn her. For her, love is only deceit and a terrible wound. The bandit allows the mother and sister to visit Mimi and take leave of her. But the vigilant Fanka spies her opportunity to slip into the house; now the outlaw is locked outside. Appearing on the balcony with the gun, Fanka fires at him wildly, in a frenzy of vengeful joy. The soldiers she has brought with her prepare to mine the wall around the house, and the outlaw runs off.

The final note is irony. One of the soldiers asks Fanka why she wished to kill the outlaw:

Fanka: I don't know! Maybe it's because I'm not so young any more, and I was sorry for...
Soldier: For what?
Fanka: My lost youth.

Perhaps the most original element in the play is the setting, a fortified house in the forest, and the situation, with its rapid reversals of the siege. All the scenes take place out of doors. Čapek realized the possibility of an outdoor staging, and even wrote some additional dialogue and directions for such a performance.

The siege motif may well date from the original version. While in Paris Čapek read with fascination newspaper accounts of how the police besieged a criminal hide-out.[3] The siege situation recurs later in *R.U.R.*, *Krakatit*, and in several other works.

A number of influences can be detected in the play. Chekhovian is the mixture of styles: comedy, farce, tragedy, and melodrama. The lyric treatment of young love certainly derives from Čapek's early period, and relates his play to those of the Czech vitalist Šrámek; the similarity is no doubt the mood of a generation. Wedekind's *Frühlings Erwachen* is probably a common source of both Čapek and Šrámek. The figure of the outlaw has something in him of Turgenev's

Bazarov or Artsybashev's Sanin. The earlier tragedy of the parents recalls Ibsen.

Perhaps the most disturbing note in the play is the mixture of realist and symbolist styles; this in itself is not a fault, to be sure, and recalls Chekhov or the early expressionism of Strindberg or Wedekind. But in Čapek's play the transitions from one style to another are handled with insufficient skill. The symbolic figure of the outlaw, nameless, coming from nowhere and going nowhere, hardly accords with the realism of the other characters, particularly with the earthy quality of Fanka, the local inhabitants, and the soldiers. Still he is vivid character, and, for all his insolence, a likable one. Disturbing too are other symbolist overtones. A gypsy fortune-teller predicts the coming tragedy. In one scene in the first act the birds converse with Mimi, twitting and chirping human speech. This is done skilfully enough: their cries are clever imitations of the sounds and cadences of bird calls. And it is possible to interpret them as senseless cries which have meaning for Mimi alone. But still the suddenness of this departure from realism is disconcerting. Another symbolist element is the metaphorical identification of blood with love. The use of verse in Act II also goes beyond realism, and provides another awkward transition.

On the other hand, the mixture of comedy and drama is handled with great skill. Still one must raise the question of how this blend of styles relates to the essential theme of the play. And here a contradiction in Čapek's conception is apparent.

Mimi loves the outlaw deeply, and we feel that she will never love another. But it is far from clear whether he loves her. Indeed, his whole nature suggests the contrary: that he is only conducting a flirtation. Even when his sympathy for her is fully aroused, he intervenes as much to defend her right to love as to win her for himself. He never commits himself to love. When he vanishes at the end, there is no suggestion that he will return, though he could come back again as easily as he had twice returned before. Indeed, the gypsy's prophecy tells us that he will not come back.

What, then, is the right of young love which Čapek is celebrating? Is it the right to commit oneself, which Mimi wants? Or is it the outlaws' right to love without restrictions, either those imposed by society or those which stem from inner responsibility? In fighting for Mimi's freedom, the hero is not serving her. It is not freedom she longs for, but a commitment of herself. Her strength is in love, not in independence.

The two viewpoints are left unresolved, and hence the final result must be tragic.[4] Čapek conceals the tragedy in the comic irony of the ending, but the tragic conclusion is inescapable. He needed to end on a comic tone, of course, if the play were actually to be a celebration of youth and love. But in fact he has cut deeper to those contradictions of human nature which often make youth and love seem an ironic waste of the gifts of life.

Still Čapek was well aware of these contradictions. In a program note to the première performance he wrote: "Just as life has changed them, just as the author too has changed, so has the conflict in *The Outlaw* changed: today the professor is more right than he was in 1911, and youth, which passes by, no longer has unlimited rights."

This clearly suggests that the play is a drama of relative points of view, that "each has his own truth." In fact there are five such "truths" in the play. There is the truth of the outlaw, who challenges the intrenched power of age in the name of youth, which does not regard consequences. There is the truth of Mimi, who wants love not as freedom, but as self-definition and self-fulfilment. There is the truth of the professor, who finds it unjust that youth, which has merited nothing, should have the best in life. There is the truth of the elder sister, for whom love is only deception. Finally, there is the truth of Fanka, who shares the professor's bitterness at the loss of youth, but does not let intellectual skepticism stay her from carrying out the duty which conventional morality imposes.

That Čapek wanted to preserve the play as a comedy, suggests that he was attempting to avoid the pessimistic implications of a relativist view of life. In *Wayside Crosses* and *Painful Tales* the pessimistic implications of relativism are at least tacitly clear. Relativism ultimately leads to an ethical chaos in which all actions are somehow "right." But Čapek tried to ignore this implication, and in the period which was to follow, he sought rather to defend relativism as a positive and optimistic type of humanism. *The Outlaw* is the dividing point between these two periods.

The strongest element in the play is its theatricality, contributed
by the setting, the rapid reversals of the siege, the rich folk-speech
of the subordinate characters, and the quick transitions from drama
to farce. Next is the lyricism of youth and love. This is the only one
of Čapek's plays which contains real poetry, not in the use of verse
or poetic prose, but as eloquence and purity of feeling. Also it is the
only one of his plays (save *The Mother*) which has a universal theme:
the conflict of youth and age. In spite of its faults, it is his best
play, perhaps his only great one. It remained his favorite throughout
the 1920s, even after later plays had won world-wide fame.

The Outlaw marks the end of the first period in Čapek's work.[5] This
is clear from the quite new, utopian themes of the works which
follow: *R.U.R.* (1921), *Factory for the Absolute* (1922), *The Makropulos Secret* (1922), *Krakatit* (1924), and *Adam the Creator* (1927).
Only the play *From the Insect World* (1920) has strong ties with the
earlier period, and this may be the result of Josef Čapek's co-
authorship. In *Painful Tales* and *The Outlaw* there are already signs
of a transition. *Painful Tales* introduced a realist style quite new
in Čapek's work, one which was to persist in his later plays and
novels, in spite of their fantastic subjects. *The Outlaw* made generous
use of colloquial speech, an innovation which the author was to
develop further in the 1920s and 1930s.

There are also internal signs of a crisis in Čapek's work at this
time. *Painful Tales* concluded with the implication that human
ethical values, relative and contradictory, provide no basis for choice.
The Outlaw continued this new ethical relativism, but with a difference which is characteristic for the second period. The relativism of
Painful Tales is frankly pessimistic; the only note of optimism is
that of sympathy, not blame, which author and readers bestow
upon these "painful" heroes. But in *The Outlaw* the pessimistic
conclusion which would follow from relativity of values is partly masked
by the comic ending. This change in tone suggests the new turn relativism was to take in Čapek's thought. Rather than pursue it to one
logical extreme, the bankruptcy of human values, he took another
tack: the discovery of the freedom, the richness, and variety of a relativist world. Thus he moved away from relativism towards pluralism.

Both relativism and pluralism are correlatives of pragmatism, and it was under the pragmatists' aegis, seemingly, that Čapek came to both philosophies. But by 1920 he had largely lost his earlier pragmatist faith.[6] This meant that he could no longer rely on the strong ethical strain contained in pragmatism. Relativism and pluralism provided him with a metaphysics, to be sure, as well as an esthetics: in his essays Čapek never tired of extolling the beauty and variety of a pluralistic world. But it was harder to ground a strong ethical teaching in relativism and pluralism. Hence the ethical and humanistic element so strong in Čapek's temperament, with its fundamental concern for the individual, was deprived of foundation.

With this philosophical imbalance there comes a decline in the quality of Čapek's work. In spite of the great popularity of *R.U.R.*, the play is artistically weaker than the earlier writings, and the works which follow are still less successful.[7] The key to this artistic decline seems to be a loss of faith in man, accompanied by desperate efforts to ground human goodness on the shaky foundation of ethical relativism. In *Factory for the Absolute* the first step towards a new ethics is taken by direct assault on the Absolute itself. In *Wayside Crosses* Čapek had given up the search for an absolute with nostalgic regret; now he attacks it as a false god, a force detrimental to life. The next logical step would have been to reassert man's innate, if relative, goodness. But the furthest Čapek can go in this direction is the cheerless conclusion that this is the best of all possible worlds *(Adam the Creator)*.

Loss of faith in man is reflected in the lack of flesh and blood in Čapek's characters during this period. He returns to the puppet as a substitute for man (insects, robots). The reality of his human figures is poorly sustained. He attempts genres such as the *roman feuilleton (Factory for the Absolute, The War with the Newts)*, melodramas *(The Makropulos Secret, Krakatit)*, or expressionist allegories *(R.U.R., Adam the Creator)*, in which the deficiencies of his character portrayal are not so apparent.

Čapek's major works of the 1920s are works of ideas, to be sure, and not of characters. But he lacks faith in the philosophical postulates behind his ingenious ideas. He does not really believe that machines will destroy man, or that modern technology will robotize him *(R.U.R.)*. He does not and cannot believe that the philosophical attitude that "life goes on" is an adequate substitute for the tragedy of individual death *(From the Insect World, The Makropulos Secret)*. He does not believe that it is enough that this is "best of all possible worlds" *(Adam the Creator)*. His new ideas are powerless, and the forms in which he symbolizes them never come alive. As a writer he was better off as a pessimist, without faith in man but with sympathy.

Only with *Hordubal* (1933) does man again take the center of the stage in Čapek's work, and this without his having elaborated a new philosophy, or even found an ingenious idea. Only when he was able to reassert faith in man, could Čapek advance artistically and philosophically. The trilogy of novels, his masterpiece, was the result.

How Čapek rescued himself from his creative dilemma and found faith in man, is of course a mystery. Suffice to say that he had followed Candide's advice and cultivated his garden. In 1925 he moved into his new house, and his passion for nature and hobbies began. A virtual withdrawal from serious literature was the result. Between 1920 and 1924 he had published two novels and three plays. From 1925 to 1933, a period twice as long, he published only one play (with Josef Čapek) and no novels. To be sure, he began to cultivate minor genres: travel books, essays, fairy tales, "hobby books," detective stories. In all of these except the last the predominant note is esthetic rather than ethical: wonder at the richness and variety of the world. Only in his detective tales (1929) does a strong ethical note and a concern for man return. These mark the beginning of the change, and the start of a third period.

9. From the Insect World

In 1920 the Brothers Čapek returned to a collaboration which had been moribund for some eight years, and wrote a comedy revue, *From the Insect World*.[1] The play was published the same year, but received its première at the National Theater only two years later, on March 8, 1922.

The inspiration for the play was suggested in part by a reading of Fabre. The brothers' conception of an insect play satirizing human vices was both original and brilliantly theatrical. True, the fable and beast epos are ancient literary genres, but this form of satire seems to be rarer in the drama. The most specific model for the Čapeks' play is a story by the Russian writer Vsevolod Garšin, "What Never Happened," a philosophical dialogue of the beasts and insects. In the Čapeks' play the figures of the dung beetle, anxiously fondling its ball of manure, and the larva, struggling to be reborn, clearly derive from Garšin's story.[2]

The authors borrowed liberally from the techniques of ballet, revue, film, and pantomime. The play provides ample opportunity for virtuoso acting, speech nuance and movement. The dialogue is colorful, with a rich variety of speech levels.

Though theatrical, the play is essentially undramatic, for the form, a series of scenes taken from the life of different insects, is that of revue and not drama. Moreover, the grotesqueness of the setting, speech, and action might well have turned the play into a spectacle divorced from human life. To unite the individual scenes, the brothers introduced a human character, a tramp, who observes the follies of insect life and comments on them. But this role is more than that of chorus; he is also protagonist, not as *actor*, however, but as *patient*. Only at the end do we discover that the action is about him and has happened to him. He forms a bridge between the audience and the spectacle itself. The tramp—as wanderer—is of course a symbolic figure. As protagonist and chorus together, he is perhaps unique in the modern theater; one must go back to the medieval mystery plays for a parallel. And in fact, the authors were fully conscious of their play's kinship to the mystery and morality dramas.

The tramp is Man. This truth is realized with superlative irony:

Tramp: Yes, that's who I am; they know me everywhere.—I am Man,[3] you see. No one calls me anything else. They say, "Man, I'll have you pinched," "Man, clear up, get it done, bring me that," or "Move along, man!" But I don't take offence because I'm a man. If I were to say. "Man, give me a dime," they'd be insulted. If they don't like it, all right then. I'll think of them as butterflies, or beetles, or ants, whatever they like.

And so we are introduced to the drama of insect life. The first act is laid in the butterfly world. Two fading beauties compete for the attentions of a young poet, who pretends to be a rake, but is at heart inordinately shy. The situation and the cynical wit remind us of *The Garden of Krakonoš* and *The Fateful Game of Love* (indeed, the poet and his beefy rival recall Gilles and Trivalin in the earlier play). Here too there is little more than the deliberate sense of the vanity and monotony of the eternal cycle of falling in and out of love.

In the second act, "The Marauders," we see the virtues and joys of family life as through a concave lens. The reverse image so obtained is that of the insularity of the family, its indifference and cruelty to outsiders, its rapacity and greed in the name of devotion to itself. The first scene is a satire on senseless accumulation of capital:

Onto the stage there rolls a great ball of manure, pushed by two beetles.
Mr. Beetle: Are you sure nothing's happened to it?
Mrs. Beetle: Just suppose! How could it! Ach, what a scare! You're all right, pretty little ball, aren't you? You're our dear little ball!
Mr. Beetle: Haha, our capital! Our dear little dung pile. Our gold! Our all!

Mrs. Beetle: You beautiful dirt, you treasure, you wonderful little ball, you priceless possession!

Mr. Beetle: Our love and our only joy! How we've saved and scraped, the dung we've carried and the stinking scraps we've snatched from our mouths to save up—

Mrs. Beetle: —and ground with our feet and the holes we've dug out, how we've raked it up, before we had it all squeezed together and piled up—

Mr. Beetle: —and rounded out and filled up, our great pretty pearl!

Mrs. Beetle: Our jewel!

Mr. Beetle: Our life!

Mrs. Beetle: Our whole creation!

Mr. Beetle: Just smell it, old woman! The beauty of it! Just weigh it! How much we have!

Mrs. Beetle: The gift of God...

Mr. Beetle: I'm crazy with joy. I... I... I'm crazy with joy. I'm really crazy.

Mrs. Beetle: Why?

Mr. Beetle: With anxiety. Now we have our ball! I've looked forward to it so, and now we have it, we must make a new one. The work it'll take!

Mrs. Beetle: Why a new one?

Mr. Beetle: Stupid! So we can have two.

Mrs. Beetle: Ah, two. That's right.

Mr. Beetle: Ha, just think of it: two balls! At least two. Let's say at least three...

Mrs. Beetle: Beetle!

Mr. Beetle: What is it?

Mrs. Beetle: I'm afraid. Somebody might steal it from us.

Mr. Beetle: What? Who?

Mrs. Beetle: Our Ball. Our joy. Our all.

Mr. Beetle: Our baaa—ll? For God's sake, don't scare me!

Mrs. Beetle: If... if... if we can't take it along with us when we're making that other one.

The cuckoo fly and the tramp discuss the responsibilities of family life:

Cuckoo Fly: Do you have children?

Tramp: No, I don't think so.

Cuckoo Fly: Ah! Have you seen her?

Tramp: Who?

Cuckoo Fly: My larva. She's beautiful, isn't she? A clever child. And how she's growing! What an appetite she has, ha ha! Children are a great joy, aren't they?

Tramp: Everyone says so.

Cuckoo Fly: Isn't it so? At least we fathers know whom we're working for. You have a child, you work hard, you fight! That's life, isn't it? A child wants to grow, it wants to "eaty," to have its goodies, to play, doesn't it? Isn't it so?

Tramp: A child demands a great deal.

Cuckoo Fly: Would you believe that I bring home two or three crickets a day?

Tramp: For whom?

Cuckoo Fly: My child. Wonderful, isn't she? And so clever! You think she eats them all up? Not at all, only the tenderest parts, while they're still alive, ha ha! An extraordinary child, don't you think?

The crickets seem an ideal couple; the husband, with his solicitous care for his pregnant wife; the wife with her domesticity and love for curtains. They find an empty house, vacated by another cricket who, impaled on a thorn, is still struggling. But they only congratulate themselves on their luck and snicker at his misfortune. Soon the cuckoo fly strikes them down. Paralyzed, the tramp witnesses this double murder. He is joined by a parasite:

Tramp: And no one cried out with horror! No one rushed to help them!

Parasite: Bravo, comrade! Just my opinion.

Tramp: To perish without any defense!

Parasite: That's what I say. I've been watching a while, but I wouldn't do that. No, I couldn't do that. Everyone wants to live, doesn't he?

Tramp: Who are you?

Parasite: Me? No one special. I'm a poor fellow. An orphan. They call me a parasite.

Tramp: Can one kill like that?

Parasite: Just what I say. You think that cuckoo fly needs them? You think he's hungry like me? Go on! He kills to stock up. He's laying in a supply. A scandal, isn't it? Is that justice? Why should he have supplies when someone else goes hungry? Because he has a dagger and I have only my bare hands? Isn't it so?

Tramp: I'd say so.

Parasite: That's what I say. There's no equality. For instance, I don't kill anyone. My jaws are too soft. I mean, my conscience is too soft.

I don't have the means of suns... sunste... sustenance. I'm just hungry.
Is that right?

Tramp: One... one... one shouldn't kill.

Parasite: My very words, comrade. Or at least you shouldn't accumulate. Eat your fill and that's enough. Accumulation is stealing from
those who don't know how to accumulate. Eat your fill and stop! Then
there would be enough for all, isn't it so?

Tramp: I don't know.

Parasite: That's what I say.

But when the cuckoo fly goes away, the parasite eats up the two
crickets and the larva herself in the bargain. Thus both capitalism
and communism are rejected.

The tramp reflects that the greed and cruelty of the marauding
insects must be due to their anarchist individualism. The authority
of the community and state is the answer. The third act takes us to
the world of the ants. But here he finds only totalitarian order, the
goal of which is greater production for war. Work tempos are increased, though the workers drop from exhaustion in their places.
The customary war slogans are paraded, and a pretext is found to
wage war on a neighboring hill of yellow ants. But the yellows win,
and destroy the whole colony. Contemptuously the tramp crushes
them with his foot.

Throughout the second and third acts a chrysalis has been
struggling to be born. Solemnly she declares that something new,
something transcendant will come into the world with her birth.
Now in the epilogue her moment arrives. A chorus of ephemerae
dance over the stage, singing the intoxication of life:

> We whirl life!
> We dance life!
> We ourselves are life!
> O Life! Life!

Their ecstatic dance endures for a moment, and one by one they
sink to the ground, dead. Now the chrysalis opens to bring forth
another ephemera, who announces that she brings "a great message"
to the world. Before she can pronounce it she too sinks to the earth.

The episode is a parody of the vitalist poetry of the brothers'
youth. Life itself is perhaps not the answer either, then, to the

tramp's quest, for itself it is meaningless unless man can give it meaning, and it only passes into death.

And now the tramp himself wrestles with death, though he begs pitifully for a respite. Two slugs observe his struggles with interest:

First Slug: Hey, shlug!
Second Slug: What?
First Slug: He'sh shtruggling with death.
Second Slug: Let'sh watch, shall we?...
Tramp: You'd choke a man who's down, you coward? Let me go, let me tell—everyone—I want just a little while—Let me—live! Just live! *(Loudly)* No! Go away! I have so many things to say yet! *(Sinks to his knees)* I know—now—how to live. *(Falls on his back)*.
First Slug: Well, he'sh done for.
Second Slug: Mershiful heavensh, what a losh. Woe, woe. Shuch a mishfortune! Why did you deshert ush?
First Slug: What are you bawling about? It ishn't any of our buishnesh.
Second Slug: But that'sh how you talk when shomeone diesh.

Morning dawns. A woodcutter appears and finds the body of the tramp. A woman comes in, carrying a child for christening.

Woodcutter: One is born and one dies.
Woman: And always there are people enough.

Thus the epilogue ends on a note of hope: life goes on in spite of death. Yet the phrase, "And always there are people enough" seems a terrible irony in the face of death. For it is man who dies, and only society which goes on. The brothers meant the ending to be optimistic, but it may sound like the final and most cynical note of all. And so the play was taken by reviewers and public all over the world. In answer to their many objectors, the brothers wrote a second ending; the director could decide which to use. In the variant ending the tramp awakes after the departure of the two slugs, to find that he had only dreamt of death. The woodcutter enters, greets him, and asks if he wants work chopping trees. The tramp joyfully accepts.

The choice of endings, therefore, is between life and work. In making such a choice the brothers may seem to have abdicated their responsibility as author, and both these answers to the tramp's question seem irrelevant. The second answer (work) had seemingly been disposed of already in Acts II and III: honest work may be perverted to selfish or self-destructive ends.

As apologists for their play, the brothers wrote a long preface to the second edition:

During its [the play's] brief existence so many friendly and hostile words have been written, that it is difficult for the authors to add anything to that confusing and many-voiced concert. Their play is "a terrible satire on love, wealth, and war," but also "an ugly, cynical and pessimistic drama, in which there is no truth" *(Christian Science Monitor)*, "a play of John the Baptist" *(Freethinker)*, and "a cruel, dirty piece of symbolism" *(Sheffield Daily Telegraph)*, "an eye-opener for frivolous spectators" and an "image of antediluvian times." "Kill them," one Berlin critic wrote about the authors, while Kerr [the critic of the *Berliner Tageblatt*] enthusiastically greeted the "first pair of brothers," and so on...

Well, to all this the authors have very little to add. They would, however, make one reservation: their comedy may be ugly, but it is not pessimistic. One American critic wrote that the spectator wonders whether he should cut his throat, if the world is as bad as it is depicted in this play. The authors entreat their audiences and readers not to do this, for it was not their intention to cut people's throats. Who the devil compels you to identify yourselves with butterflies or beetles, with crickets or ants or ephemerae? Because these creatures are depicted as loafers and self-seekers, as scoundrels and libertines, militarists and parasites, does it therefore follow that they denote people? Does the demonstration that private, family, or state selfishness is petty, insect-like, brutal and lousy, prove that everything human is lousy? Is there not at least one human being opposed to the insects, the tramp, a creature who sees all, judges and searches for a way? Each spectator or reader may attempt to see himself in the wandering tramp; instead of that— disquieted or scandalized—he has taken it for granted that it is his own image or the image of his society which he sees in these vermin, which in fact do represent—true, with a deliberate bias—certain vices. And just this optical illusion is a testimony that the authors did not write their "ugly and cynical" satire in vain.

They did not intend to write a drama, but a mystery in a quite antiquated and naive sense. Just as in the medieval mystery play there appeared personifications of Avarice, Egotism, or Virtue, so certain moral concepts are here personified as insects, simply for greater edification. True, Virtue is absent here; if the authors, say, had introduced on their stage a bee as an incarnation of Obedience, or a spider as a personification of Modesty, their piece would no doubt have seemed less pessimistic. If they did not do so, they had their reasons: the mirror which they held up to life was intentionally and tendentiously crooked, and would have distorted the mug of even the fairest of human Virtues. And lo, their malevolent trick succeeded beyond all expectation, and people without number *recognized* man in that distorted grotesque and realized that there is something ugly, brutal, and worthless even where they were not accustomed to look for it. We did not write about people or about the vermin of the field; we wrote about certain vices. And, God knows, it is not dirty pessimism to find that vice is something wretched and lousy. Of course it is not elevating or original, either, but *that* was really not our end.

And so those who called the comedy a "worn-out allegory" were right after all. Good heavens, it is terribly worn out, bought, so to speak, from a dealer in second-hand clothing, and then turned once more; but believe us, it is hard to preach morality in a dinner jacket; the morality of dinner jackets would have appeared essentially different from what we wanted to tell people in this play.

In a letter to the editor of the *New York Herald* the brothers added:

You, the public of our play, you are neither butterflies, beetles, nor ants if you can see the futility of insect life; you yourself are *Tramps;* you are the living, enduring, truth-seeking consciences, just like our own *Tramp*. His life was sad only because he remained in the play alone... and this is our pessimistic error, for we too were composing our play in solitude; but if the *Tramp* knew that in other woods—for instance, American woods—other *Tramps* were erring and seeking as he was, he would have bequeathed them his endless quest. For our insect play has another epilogue, printed but as yet not performed on the stage... This epilogue in the book edition was written with a deep recollection of your philosopher, William James, whose name is surely a charm against pessimism.[4]

The reader can only agree with the authors that a satire of vice is not pessimistic as such. But this argument hardly disposes of the fundamental problem. The question is not whether vice exists, or even whether virtue and vice may at times actually be opposite faces of the same coin, as the second act suggests. Rather it is how should man live in a world where moral standards are relative? How does one choose when the good of one's family conflicts with the good of society? The tramp finds his answer to this question only when he dies.

Is the failure to give an answer to this question not pessimism? Perhaps there is an escape, after all. Life is not the answer, but the process, the search for an answer. That the question has no ready answer is one of the countless facts of life itself, which man must accept.

Hence the play ends on a note of ambiguity. From here it was possible for Karel Čapek to pursue relativism in one of two directions: as a final answer to all questions, which would ultimately have led him to pessimism; or as a working technique in the search for truth. He himself warned against the first solution when he wrote:

I do not wish to play with words, but if I have ever said that all is relative, then something quiet unrelativistic has slipped out of me, for that sinful word "all" smells of a buried and concealed absolutism... A true, hundred-percent relativism must achieve a finer distinction: almost all is relative.[5]

10. Will Man Survive:
Robots and Newts

R.U.R., or "Rossum's Universal Robots," had its première at the National Theater in Prague on January 25, 1921.[1] Within several years, the play was translated and performed in most of the countries of Europe, as well as in the United States and Japan. Čapek's name (in various mispronounced and even misspelled forms) became a household word, along with the term "robot" itself. This word, coined by Josef Čapek, is derived from the Czech *robota*, "forced labor," "servitude."[2]

The title of the play, *R.U.R.* or "Rossum's Universal Robots," is the name of a fictitious corporation, and is in English in the original. This would suggest a British or American setting for the play. But the names of the characters are multi-national; here as often later, Čapek tried to create a deliberately international background for his theme. A number of references are made in the play to the commercial interests of Europe, and there is no suggestion that America or Britain alone is guilty of a technological revolution which might submerge the human race.

The idea of a robot, an artificial man, is of course very old. One source is the Jewish legend of the Golem of Prague, which turned against those who misused its sacred power. Mary Shelley's novel *Frankenstein* is another manifest source, closer in that both the robot and Frankenstein's monster are creations not of magic, but of modern technology. Certain details of Old Rossum's experiments, as well as the island setting, may have been suggested by H. G. Wells's novel, *The Island of Dr. Moreau,* in which a scientist operates on animals to make them more nearly resemble men. In Čapek's own work, the robot finds a prototype in the puppets of the early tales.

Nor was Čapek the first to introduce an artificial man on the stage, as is sometimes claimed. Goethe's *Faust,* Part II, is of course no more a play than its Homunculus is really an artificial man. But the mechanical dolls of Delibes' ballet *Coppélia* (1870) and Offenbach's opera *The Tales of Hoffmann* (1881) are earlier examples of stage puppets.

What is new in Čapek's play is the complex meaning of the symbol of the robot, which represents not only the machine and its power to free man from toil but, at the same time, symbolizes man himself, dehumanized by his own technology. From the technical point of view, man is an inefficient instrument, whose emotional and spiritual life only impedes the drive of modern technology. Either he must give way to the machine, or he himself must become a machine. This aspect of the symbol we have already found in the brothers' early story, "The System" (1908). Last, the robot symbolizes man dehumanized by the very freedom from toil which the machine assures him; gone are the struggle of life and the challenge to man's spirit. In *R.U.R.* man loses even his ability to reproduce, the last thing which distinguishes him from the robot. The complexity of the robot symbol must be realized for a proper understanding of Čapek's play. He was too honest a writer to create a superficial melodrama about man-like machines which revolt against man— though this is obviously the aspect of the play which made it so popular.

Another influence on the technological theme of *R.U.R.* was Georg Kaiser's *Gas,* Part I (1918). In both dramas man is seen as an imperfect instrument from the technological point of view: in Kaiser's play the workers become mere expressionistic embodiments of hands or feet, in accordance with the task they must perform at their machines. In *R.U.R.* man's soul is described as standing in the way of mechanical perfection: man plays the violin, goes for walks, and has children—all impediments to his role as an integer in the modern world of industry and commerce. In both plays technology reaches a limit of the irrational which it cannot control: in Kaiser the formula for gas is calculated perfectly, yet the gas explodes; in Čapek, the formula creates mere robots, but in the end robots become men. Man's spirit cannot be regimented, Čapek is saying, even by misapplication of his own reason and science. This theme also reminds us of the brothers' earlier story, "The Luminous Depths."

Both plays end in the apparent victory of technology over spirit: in Kaiser the workers reject the hero's efforts to humanize them; in Čapek, man is destroyed by his own robots. But in both spirit is actually the victor: in *Gas*, the hero has discovered man's true nature—life—and realizes that others, too, will find it; in *R.U.R.*, the robots live and reproduce.

R.U.R. differs strikingly from Kaiser's play, however, in its strong defense of technological utopia—the dream of the factory manager Domin. Kaiser's engineer offers little more to the workers than a picture of a world in which they will have new toys to play with.

Kaiser's play is thoroughly expressionistic in style, while Čapek has blended expressionism with realism. In fact, only the figure of the robot itself (and the final transformation of robots into men) is expressionistic; otherwise Čapek's treatment is conventional and realistic. This mixture of styles was hardly a concession to popular appeal, for it was just the expressionistic symbol of the robot which made the play so popular. What Čapek was seeking, rather, was a humanization of the play, and in this he at least partly succeeded. Today Kaiser's *Gas* seems totally lifeless, while *R.U.R.*, for all its sins against the stage, remains moving and human. Still, in its purity of style, Kaiser's play is surely the more consistent.

R.U.R. opens with a "comedy prologue." Helena Glory, daughter of the president of the firm of Rossum's Universal Robots, comes to visit the island where robots are manufactured. Her ostensible motive is curiosity, but actually she intends to incite the robots to revolt and claim equality with men. All this is quite useless, the directors of the factory assure her, for the robots do only what they are told and have no conception of abstract justice or equality. All the men on the island fall in love with her, and finally she accepts the proposal of Domin, the managing director.

The expository section of the Prologue introduces us to two contrasting aspects of the robot symbol. Their inventor, Old Rossum (the name is derived from Czech *rozum*, "reason") was a rationalist who sought to create life as a proof of the nonexistence of God. He had no interest in the economic exploitation of his discovery. For this type of scientist Čapek always had the warmest praise, though he was fully aware of the limitations of such a point of view. Elsewhere he has described the great scientists of the past as "adventurers and romantics of intellectual discovery," and "Don Quixotes of the nineteenth century."[3] They had the courage of their convictions; their dreams, even their challenges to God, were proud assertions of the human spirit. In his zeal for pure science Old Rossum had striven to create man with everything Nature had given him— even an appendix. It was his nephew, rather, who simplified his discovery, created the robot, and set up manufacture on a mass-production basis.

The "comedy" element of the Prologue arises from Helena's inability to distinguish robots from humans. In one scene she refuses to believe that a robot is not a woman; later she mistakes the directors of the factory for robots, and tries to incite them to revolt. The humor here is not gratuitous; it introduces us directly to the theme of the play. The point is that man is already dehumanized, and so Helena cannot tell the difference. Hence Domin insists that he can afford to wait no more than five minutes for Helena's reply to his proposal of marriage; he has become a prisoner of his own dream of technological utopia.

The Prologue is set apart from the body of the play because it is comedy, while the play proper is drama. Act I is the kernel of *R.U.R.;* in fact, the dramatic conflict is essentially resolved by its finish, and what follows is largely anticlimax.[4] In this act we learn that robots all over the world have risen against their masters, and that man is doomed. We also learn that man has lost his power to reproduce his kind. Revolted by this news, Helena burns the manuscript of Rossum's formula. But in so doing she destroys herself and those she loves, for the manuscript could have served as the bargaining price for their freedom.

Once we know that man has lost his ability to reproduce, and that the robots have risen against him, the outcome is obvious. Yet Čapek delays the inevitable ending by introducing an electrified barrier which the robots cannot cross until they have taken the factory power plant. This delay is dramatically necessary; otherwise the play would be over by the end of the first act. (Here of course is the reason why Acts II and III seem anticlimactic.) The author needed time to comment on what was happening if the play were to be a drama of ideas, and not a mere melodrama. In the Prologue and Act I the whole burden of argument is against technology. Such an opposition of black and white was foreign to Čapek's purpose. There is no reason to suppose, as some critics have, that he was opposed to human inventiveness as such; in fact, several of his essays welcome new inventions.[5] Moreover, Čapek was a relativist. Domin too has a share of the truth in his dream of a world in which man is freed of toil and his energies are released to pursue the things of the spirit. This dream is depicted in the second act.

Of course, Domin could have described his dream in Act I, and the robots could have launched their attack during Act II. This would have been the more conventional dramatic procedure. But it would have deprived the author of a solemn moment in the symbolic plane of the drama: the awful realization that mankind is passing from the earth.

Čapek later wrote that he conceived *R.U.R.* as a eulogy to man, that he wanted to view human life in retrospect and say, as Hallemeier does in the play, "It was a great thing to be a man." And Čapek adds: "Technology, progress, ideals, faith—all these were rather only illustrations of humanity than the sense of the play."[6]

Of course Čapek exaggerates here; the note of eulogy is not the final one. The end of the play is the miracle of life, the transformation of robots into men. But even if his dramatic means are questionable, Čapek was right to introduce this philosophical note into his play. For the threat to man's existence can be meaningful only if the spectator really grasps that man is about to pass from the earth, if he comprehends what a "great thing" it was "to be a man."

The delay of the electrified screen is also necessary if man is to understand *why* he is doomed to destruction, why the robots have revolted against him. Dr. Gall confesses that he has modified the robots' sensitivity to please Helena. Their coldness had terrified her, and she sought to give them a soul. To gratify her, Gall has increased the "nervous irritability" of the robots. It is this, seemingly, which has produced the revolt. But Gall's hypothesis is far from certain; perhaps it is the fact that there are more robots than people, and the robots are stronger and more intelligent. Perhaps it is because the robots were given arms to fight in national wars. Or perhaps it is because man forgot to create robots with national differences which would turn them against one another. Only at the end of the act do we discover the true cause of the robots' hatred for mankind; they are man's equals, but they work, while man does not.

Both capitalism and communism must share the responsibility for the robot uprising. It is not technology which destroys man, the directors conclude at one point, but greed for profits and the inevitable law of supply and demand. And when Domin reads a manifesto addressed to "robots of the world," he asks who taught them such phrases. Here the robot uprising appears as a symbol of socialist revolution; may not man forfeit even his own humanity to gain a materialist utopia, whether achieved through capitalism or socialism?

The second act culminates in the end of the siege and the massacre of the defenders. The robots kill everyone except the construction engineer, Alquist, who is spared because he still works with his hands.

Act III is also a dramatic anticlimax, but it likewise is necessary for the philosophical point of the play. Alquist is alone, the only human spared by the robots. In despair at man's passing, he tries to discover the secret of manufacturing life. The robot leaders order him to dissect live robots. He attempts this, but his nervous hands cannot hold the scalpel. As he mourns his lack of resoluteness, he observes that his two robot servants, Primus and Helena, have fallen in love. Alquist puts their feeling to the test by suggesting that he intends to dissect one of them. Each begs to be taken in place of the other. Alquist tells them to go and be man and wife to one another. He reads from Genesis how God created man and woman in His own image. "Life will not perish," he concludes.

Ideologically the play thus turns in a circle, denying the very thesis it had asserted for dramatic purposes. This thesis, that modern civilization threatens to destroy man by removing the element of struggle from life, is contradicted: life and love will not perish. This contradiction is no inconsistency, but a deliberate use of a false dramatic resolution followed by the true one. This is why the construction of *R.U.R.*, with its two acts of apparent anticlimax, is so unorthodox.

On June 21, 1923, a public discussion was held in London on the meaning of *R.U.R.* Shaw, Chesterton, and Commander Joseph Kenworthy were among the participants. Shaw made some amusing remarks on the robot element in human nature: man must spend a great part of his life a slave to routine, whether or not it is imposed by modern technology. Better a bit more routine, a bit more "robotry," in order to give man more time for greater spiritual independence, Shaw concluded. Chesterton considered the play an eloquent satire on the irresponsibility of modern capitalist civilization. Kenworthy saw in *R.U.R.* a warning against the threat of war and international anarchy. Such interpretations of the play as these last two are popular, and in a sense obvious. Čapek took exception to them, however, and published a rebuttal in *The Saturday Review;*

I have just learnt of the discussion about the meaning of a play which, for certain serious reasons, I lay claim to as my own. Authors are reputed to be childishly vain, and as one of them I claim the privilege of saying a few words on behalf of my work.

Mr. Chesterton, in the course of the discussion, said rightly that nobody can say what is the tendency of a work of art. I cannot tell it myself. But the discussion was by no means useless, in that it gave an opportunity to the distinguished participators to express their personal opinions, creeds and ideals. I enjoyed very much the creeds and ideals of Mr. Chesterton, as well as those of Mr. Shaw and Commander Kenworthy. But it seems to me that, so far as my play was concerned, their chief interest was centred upon Robots. For myself, I confess that as the author I was much more interested in men than in Robots.

There are some fathers who are, shall we say, more interested in education in general than in that of their own children in particular. Allow me to take the opposite view, of a father who speaks of his own child rather than of the principles of education. I am not altogether sure of what I have written, but I know very well what I wished to write. I wished to write a comedy, partly of science, partly of truth. The old inventor, Mr. Rossum (whose name in English signifies Mr. Intellect or Mr. Brain), is no more or less than a typical representative of the scientific materialism of the last century. His desire to create an artificial man—in the chemical and biological, not the mechanical sense—is inspired by a foolish and obstinate wish to prove God to be unnecessary and absurd. Young Rossum is the modern scientist, untroubled by metaphysical ideas; scientific experiment is to him the road to industrial production, he is not concerned to prove, but to manufacture. To create a Homunculus is a mediaeval idea; to bring it in line with the present century this creation must be undertaken on the principle of mass-production. Immediately we are in the grip of industrialism; this terrible machinery must not stop, for if it does it would destroy the lives of thousands. It must, on the contrary, go on faster and faster, although it destroy in the process thousands and thousands of other existences. Those who think to master the industry are themselves mastered by it; Robots must be produced although they are, or rather *because* they are, a war industry. The conception of the human brain has at last escaped from the control of human hands. This is the comedy of science.

Now for my other idea, the comedy of truth. The General Manager Domin, in the play, proves that technical progress emancipates man from hard manual labour, and he is quite right. The Tolstoyan Alquist, on the contrary, believes that technical progress demoralizes him, and I think he is right, too. Bussman thinks that industrialism alone is capable of supplying modern needs; he is right. Ellen is instinctively afraid of all this inhuman machinery, and she is profoundly right. Finally, the Robots themselves revolt against all these idealists, and, as it appears, they are right, too.

We need not look for actual names for these various and controverted idealisms. Be these people either Conservatives or Socialists, Yellows or Reds, the most important thing is—and this is the point I wish particularly to stress—that all of them are right in the plain and moral sense of the word. Each and every one of them has the deepest reasons, material and mental, for his beliefs, and according to his lights seeks the greatest happiness for the greatest possible number of his fellow-men. I ask whether it is not possible to see in the present social conflict of the world an analogous struggle between two, three, five, equally serious verities and equally generous idealisms? I think it is possible, and this is the most dramatic element in modern civilization, that a human truth is opposed to another truth no less human, ideal against ideal, positive worth against worth no less positive, instead of the struggle being, as we are so often told it is, one between noble truth and vile selfish error.

These are the things I should like to have said in my comedy of truth, but is seems that I failed, for none of the distinguished speakers who took part in the discussion have discovered this simple tendency in "R.U.R."[7]

Thus Čapek denies that the play is concerned only with the menace of technology to modern society. The danger, in fact, is civilization itself, which threatens to overwhelm man by its sheer weight and impersonality. Human reason has created civilization, but is manifestly unable to control it.

As Čapek states, the second idea of the play is that of the "comedy of truth," the conflict of pieces of relativist truth, each of them in itself quite valid. There are four such points of view expressed in the play. Domin stands for man as master of the universe (indeed, his name implies this); his is the dream of freedom for man from toil. Opposed to him is Nána, Helena's old nurse, a peasant woman of strict religious persuasion. For her "all inventions are against the Lord God." A more sophisticated variant of her belief is presented by Alquist, the construction engineer. Though he is not certain whether God exists, he recognizes the importance of spirit and moral law, and he prays. He has an almost Tolstoyan faith in work. His profession symbolizes his creativity, which for him is the inner goal of the human need to work. But Alquist forgets that work and creativity are not the same; the drudgery from which Domin seeks to liberate man is not the longing to create.

Alquist's character is developed through an interesting literary reference to Ibsen's *Master Builder:*

Helena: What do you do when you feel worried?
Alquist: I lay brick. I take off my engineer's coat, and climb up on the scaffolding...
Helena: And don't you feel dizzy on the scaffold?
Alquist: No. You don't know how good it feels to hold a brick in your hand, to set it down and knock it into place.

Ibsen's Solness is proud, and feels dizzy because he fears he will fall. Alquist is humble, and climbs the scaffold to do humble work.

Finally, there is Helena's viewpoint. Her name, which is also that of the beautiful robot girl, symbolizes her nature as eternal woman. She acts instinctively, out of feeling, not reason. But she too is doomed, for she does no work, and, though she desires children, she does not have them.

The chief fault in the interplay of these four points of view is that there is no acceptable ideology to counter that of Domin, only the logic of events themselves. Nána's viewpoint, stolidly opposed to all invention as a presumption against God, would return man to an animal existence. Alquist's philosophy of creative work is a personal faith, for not every man is born to create. Helena's intuitive approach to right and wrong has no objective foundation. Though she is in touch with life, she is cut off, paradoxically, from reality, and it is her well-intentioned destruction of the manuscript which brings her own end and the end of those she loves.

The American critic Kenneth Burke has observed that *R.U.R.* fails primarily because of a lack of eloquence.[8] The intensity of Čapek's ideas is never matched by a corresponding intensity of language. Perhaps Čapek feared to depart too far from everyday speech; here the realistic and expressionistic sides of his play are in conflict. Only the ideas of Domin and Alquist approach eloquence in statement. But Domin's eloquence is sterile, for the logic of events is against him. Alquist's ideas are personal, and stand apart from the drama. Helena, who ought to be the most eloquent person in the play, is the least so. Her speeches have an almost painful banality, while her actions, such as the destruction of the manuscript, appear even more stupid. As one critic has observed, the spectator may conclude from the way the play is constructed that man disappears from the earth because Helena cannot mind her own business.[9]

From the standpoint of realism, there are other faults in the play. It seems impossible that Rossum's manuscript should exist in only one copy. Nor is it likely that Helena should be the only woman on the island, when the men there are well paid. In his need to find a symbol of sterility, Čapek sacrificed probability to the expressionist side of the play. Indeed, may not this picture suggest the existence of psychic conflict within the author himself: an island where six men live with one woman in Platonic love, and where there are no children, only robots? May not the robot symbol have had its origin in a personal fear of sterility?

Čapek was aware of the defects of *R.U.R.*, and liked it least of all his plays. In an interview with Dorothy Thompson he confessed that he was unable to comprehend what people saw in *R.U.R.* But he declined to say what was wrong with it, observing only that the spectator can see for himself. "It is a play that anyone might have written," he added. For years he refused to go to see *R.U.R.*, and gave in only when trapped in a small Czech town by the director of the local theater.[10]

How discerning a prophet was Čapek in *R.U.R.?* If the question touches only man's ability to live with technology and the machine, then his fears were in a sense exaggerated. In spite of the unprecedented rate of technological progress in our times, modern man has demonstrated his ample powers of adaptation. The specter of technological unemployment has largely been dispelled by the discovery that new machines create new responsibilities and new jobs, and by the opening of new areas of employment in personal services. And it can hardly be said that technological "utopia" has decreased the element of toil or conflict in life, as Čapek feared it might; no one is busier than the contemporary American family dwelling in suburbia. If mere survival is easier today than ever before, then the achievement of wealth and prestige costs at least as much in competitive struggle as ever.

But man's ability to adapt does not in itself guarantee his survival. The terrible destructive powers which modern science has created reopen the question and point to the very dilemma of the conflict of motives about which Čapek wrote. Čapek's robots are symbols of modern civilization as a whole. The marvellous instrument of science and technology is only a tool in the grip of uncontrolled forces: the profit motive, supply and demand, competition for markets, the mutual antipathy of nations, the armament race. Modern technology can supply instruments and weapons to serve these forces, but it cannot control them. And it is not only the conflict within man which is at fault, Čapek implies; reason itself errs when it blithely ignores these forces. Reason can forge new weapons of destruction; reason can also fabricate Domin's great dream; reason can create a socialist utopia at the price of dehumanizing man. But reason forgets that it is no absolute, that it is only the servant of the irrational in man, not the master. Reason ought to content itself with a humbler role: to restrain the conflicting forces of civilization, rather than to arm them with new weapons.

The question is of course complicated by the double answer which Čapek gives: man will be destroyed, and he will not be. Today, when the human race still survives, but scarcely knows how long it will go on surviving, it is possible to appreciate the wisdom of this ambiguous answer.

In spite of the faults of *R.U.R.*, it is safe to say that no other play on modern technology has so captured the public's imagination. Perhaps, in view of the great urgency of its theme, it has a just claim to be Čapek's most popular work.

The subject of *R.U.R.* might seem more suitable for a novel, since the novel is the traditional form of utopian literature. Apparently Čapek himself came to this conclusion. His next major work, *Factory for the Absolute* (1922), was a utopian novel. And fifteen years after *R.U.R.*, he produced a novel on a variant of the robot theme, *The War with the Newts* (1936).[11]

The War with the Newts is Čapek's greatest work in the utopian genre. Closer to Swift than to Wells,[12] it has a satirical tone absent in *R.U.R.*, and is far less melodramatic. Like the earlier *Factory for the Absolute*, the novel is a *roman feuilleton*, and it too appeared serially in *Lidové noviny*. The loose form of the *roman feuilleton* allowed Čapek great freedom for satire and parody. The novel is a brilliant pastiche of the most diverse kinds of writing: newspaper articles, memoirs, scholarly works, manifestoes, etc. Every conceivable typographic device is employed for comic or satiric effect; there is even an obscure historical note printed in the older Czech type *(švabach)*, as well as an extremely blurred and tiny photograph of the giant newts.

Unlike *R.U.R.*, *The War with the Newts* makes no pretense at realism, and hence there is nothing to conflict with the free play of Čapek's fantasy. In *R.U.R.* the unity of setting, dialogue, and action,

as well as the dramatic form itself—all suggest a realism at variance
with the subject. In *The War with the Newts*, on the other hand, the
unreality of the theme never disturbs the reader. True, there is some
unevenness in the quality of different parts of the novel, but this
is inevitable in a *roman feuilleton*. More disturbing is the frequent
change in point of view. The author poses as a historian who re-
constructs the story of the newts from documents. But sometimes
he intrudes to comment on the events which he is narrating. The
author himself cannot tell us whether the human race will survive
the "war" or not, though the "historian" who studies the sources
must already know the answer, which for him lies in the past.

The idea for the novel was borrowed from Pierre Mac Orlan's
story, "La Bête conquérante" (1920).[13] In Mac Orlan's narrative a
farmer in the act of slaughtering a pig unwittingly performs a delicate operation on the animal's brain which enables it to speak. Soon
animals are trained on a scale to serve as slaves and perform
human tasks. But man, no longer compelled to work, degenerates,
and the animals revolt and take over the world.

Čapek's satirical conception is strikingly similar. In *R.U.R.* he
had already warned man of the danger which freedom from toil
might bring to human society. Like the robots of *R.U.R.*, Čapek's
newts are a more complex symbol than Mac Orlan's talented sheep
and pigs. The newts stand not only for technology's capacity to free
man from toil, but also symbolize man debased by his own civilization. In the Epilogue to the first book edition of the novel, Čapek
emphasized this relationship between the world of newts and present-
day civilization:

The critics have called it [*The War with the Newts*] a utopian novel. I do
not like that word. There is no utopia here, only the present. There is no
speculation about the future, but a mirroring of that which exists and
the surroundings in which we live. It was no matter of fantasy,... but
reality. I cannot help it; literature which is not concerned with reality
and what is actually going on in the world, which does not react as
strongly as word and idea possibly can—such literature is not my
concern.

Of course Čapek's objections need not prevent us from calling the
novel "utopian" as a convenience of literary classification. Most

serious "utopian" novels are actually anti-utopian, and present the world of the future as a background against which to project certain harmful traits of the present. Čapek's objection to the term was a response to critics who saw in the novel only fantasy. Thus he makes it abundantly clear that the world of the newts is an allegory of the contemporary world. The newts are men, but men dehumanized by the pressures of modern civilization, by technology, war, and by a false ideal of equality. A philosopher of history in the novel (modeled on Spengler) comments on this egalitarian ideal:

There is no doubt that the world of Newts will be happier than the human world has been; it will be united, homogeneous, and ruled by the same spirit. One Newt will not differ from another in speech, opinions, faith, or even in his demands on life. There will be neither cultural nor class differences, but only a division of labor. No one will be a master or a slave, but all will serve only the Great Newt Whole, which will be god, ruler, employer and spiritual leader. There will be but one race and one level.

This sounds as if the target of Čapek's satirical attack were totalitarianism, and no doubt he had both the fascist and communist super-states in mind when he wrote this passage. But the capitalist democracies, with their greed and selfish indifference to the fate of other nations, come in for an equal share of Čapek's satire. Not totalitarianism alone, but the modern delusion that mass is superior to quality, is the keynote to man's present plight. Čapek comments in the novel:

What is civilization but the ability to use that which some one else has discovered? Even if we admit that the Newts have no ideas of their own, they are quite capable of formulating their own science. True, they have no music or literature, but they get along perfectly without them, and people are beginning to discover that this is wonderfully "modern" on their part... Never in the history of mankind has so much been produced, been built or so many profits been made as in this great era... With the Newts there has come into the world a titanic progress and an ideal which is called Quantity... The Newts are simply the Multitude; their epoch-making achievement is in the number there are of them.

In this passage Čapek shows clearly (*pace* his Communist critics) that he was always an individualist; for him culture is an individual

creation, equally foreign to a totalitarian order and to the impersonal
soulless colossi of the democratic West.

The novel opens with the discovery of a species of gigantic newts
off the coast of Sumatra. At first they attract the attention of pearl
fishers, for the newts gladly exchange pearls for knives with which
to defend themselves against sharks. The intelligent newts soon
learn human speech, and prove themselves able to perform almost
any human task. Their only limitation is that they must live near
the water. A gigantic slave trade is organized; newts are employed
in harbors, docks and industrial enterprises. They build huge
factories underneath the ocean, exchanging their products for raw
materials from the earth. Humanitarians denounce the slave trade
and demand equality for the newts, but most men are simply indifferent, or more than content to exploit the newts' labor. The
powers employ armies of newts to wage wars against one another.
But soon the newts outnumber man. Multiplying rapidly, they
demand the right to extend the coast by cutting into huge areas of
mainland. Frightened, the powers offer to let them flood central
China. But the newts are not satisfied with such a compromise, and
soon they inundate half of Europe.

At this point Čapek breaks off the narrative without a resolution.
In the final chapter, the author asks himself whether the newts will
indeed take over the world, and man will perish. He cannot say. The
newts need as much coast as possible; certainly they will leave long
strips of land on which some people will survive, if only as slaves to
the newts. Perhaps the newts will begin to fight one another; in this
war so much poison will be poured into the waters that all the newts
will perish.

The novel makes a number of anti-Nazi gibes: Chief Salamander,
the dictator of the newts, is actually a human being, a German
sergeant from World War I named Andreas Schultze. Such satirical
thrusts led some critics to interpret the book as an attack on Nazism.
But the novel as a whole will not support such a view. Never does
the author suggest that the struggle is one between "good" humans
and "bad" newts; indeed, it is man who is evil in his exploitation of
the newts. There is nothing in the story of the discovery of the newts
or the trade in newt slaves to parallel the formation of the Nazi

Party or the rise of Hitler. The novel cannot be read as an allegory on Nazism alone; it is an allegory of contemporary civilization, of which Nazism is a part.

It is capitalism, in fact, which comes in for the major share of Čapek's satire, presumably because he knew it at closer range, and because he assumed that it would continue to dominate Western Europe and America. This has led contemporary critics in Czechoslovakia and the Soviet Union to read the novel purely as a satirical attack on capitalism. But this again distorts and simplifies the book's meaning. In fact, national socialism, monopolistic capitalism, and communism are all objects of Čapek's satire, for they are all self-styled absolutisms, forms of titanism which lead to loss of freedom and of that divergence among individuals and peoples which for him is the essence of human culture.[14]

The War with the Newts lacks the vitalist optimism of *R.U.R.* Man may survive—if the newts destroy themselves. But the newts *are* men. If the oceans are poisoned and they all perish, it can only be a clear warning that modern means for waging war are so perfect that with them man could achieve total destruction. This pessimistic turn reflects the passage of fifteen years. In 1920, when Čapek wrote *R.U.R.*, he had seen how man survived the horror of World War I. In 1936, the coming of a second world war was almost a certainly, and there was talk of the possible use of gas to destroy whole civilian populations. It was impossible to be certain of man's ultimate survival.

The War with the Newts is Čapek's masterpiece as utopian allegory. As a symbol the newt may not be quite so imaginative or appropriate to the author's purpose as the robot had been. But Čapek's choice was considered, as he observes in the Epilogue. In choosing the newt as an antagonist to man, he was seeking to remind man that he is not master of the Universe; Life and Nature are greater than man, and do not need him for their purposes. Neither man, nor human society, nor civilization is an absolute. Has not modern man best demonstrated this through his failure to master himself?

11. A Preview of Atomic Fission:
Two Novels of the Absolute

In 1922 Čapek published his first novel, *Factory for the Absolute*.[1]
The work appeared in thirty weekly installments in the newspaper
Lidové noviny. The author planned the novel as a serial, with a
relatively loose unity, frequent changes of characters and styles, and
much journalistic commentary.

Factory for the Absolute continues the anti-utopian tradition of
R.U.R., though in a lighter vein. At the same time it constitutes
Čapek's first attempt to preach relativism as a self-sufficient, positive
philosophy.

The point of departure for the novel is a brilliant anticipation of
later developments in atomic physics. An engineer develops a process
for the industrial utilization of atomic energy. But the invention
has one drawback: the annihilation of matter brings the release of
the spiritual energy of the Absolute which pervades matter. The
released Absolute has a powerful effect on all who are in the vicinity
of the process. They undergo religious conversion, experience
ecstasies and trance states, prophesy, perform miracles, etc. At first
the Church refuses to have anything to do with the new discovery;
its function is not "to bring God into the world," as the astute
Bishop Linda patiently explains, "but rather to control and regulate
Him." But in spite of this circumspect advice, business men insist
on marketing the Carburator, as the invention is called, with
disastrous consequences. The whole economic system at once breaks

down. Those who are converted give away their property to their fellows, and begin to preach or make pilgrimages. At the same time the Absolute itself takes over production. Soon there is such an abundance of goods that they lose all value, and are no more worth selling than sand or sea water. Factories are surrounded by huge piles of manufactured wares, while a few miles distant there is acute scarcity.

In each country the Absolute seems to manifest itself differently— in accord with Čapek's doctrine of relativism. In America He goes in for sports. In England He is a conservative. In France He is anti-clerical and even rationalistic. Each people claims Him for itself. Fanaticism is rampant, and a series of devastating religious wars breaks out. In Europe there is a Catholic crusade against the Protestants, and a war between pope and anti-pope. In America the main struggle is between the Wets and the Drys, while the Japanese invade the West Coast. Asia and Central Europe are inundated by yellow hordes. In France a corporal named Bobinet is inspired to rid the land of the Carburators. In gratitude the people crown him emperor, and he undertakes a series of campaigns which take him as far as India. There he disappears, in search of the fabulous land of the Amazons.

At last the madness passes, and life returns to normal. The last Carburators are destroyed. In the final scene a few of the characters of the novel meet at a tavern to eat sausages, drink beer, and comment on what has happened. Man tries to believe dogmas— absolutes—they agree, and refuses to have faith in other men and their right to believe something different. Faith in man is more important than faith in ideas.

The critics were unfavorably impressed by the novel, though they admitted that the idea and the first chapters were brilliant. The London *Times* found the conception striking—one which "might have been a Wellsian idea, treated in a Chestertonian manner." But it could not praise the execution.[2] The main weakness, as Václav Černý pointed out, is a lack of unity and direction in the work after the twelfth chapter. The novel falls apart at the middle, and the later installments could be interchanged at random.[3] In fact, the first twelve chapters are witty and original, full of extravagant

humor and well-drawn characters. What follows them, however, is
rather labored chronicle of world events consequent on the exploitation of the new discovery. This chronicle owes not a little in its
satirical conception to Anatole France's *Penguin Island.*

Čapek was conscious of the work's unevenness, and in the second
collected edition he added an apologetic preface. The first twelve
chapters, he explained, had been written on vacation, in a single,
energetic burst. These were sent off to *Lidové noviny* with a definite
promise to complete the work. When the twelve chapters ran out,
Čapek was hard put to it to keep ahead of the paper's constant
demand for installments.

We may grant that Čapek's preachments in the novel are not very
subtle. It is clear, however, from the circumstances of the novel's
creation and publication that he never intended it to be taken as a
major work. Nevertheless he defended the novel for its philosophy:

> All of *Factory for the Absolute* is animated by the philosophy of relati-
> vism; a philosophy which is neither very new nor uplifting, a philosophy
> which I repeat *ad nauseam* in my books... For me it is the only path by
> which it is possible to come to love for man when we have lost our faith
> in humanity; the only way to come to a love for the search for truth when
> we cannot find truth; to unite the most shameful skepticism with a
> naive and effective trust...
>
> Each man who believes in some sort of Truth thinks that therefore
> he must hate and kill a man who believes in a Truth which carries a
> different brand name... Man is something more valuable than his
> "truth."[4]

Čapek's critics also charged that the novel lacked unity, since it
had two diverse themes. One is the theme of the Absolute as a
religious force which gets in the way of life. The other is the folly
of a utopia in which man does no work, for the Absolute itself takes
over production.[5] These two subjects are seemingly unrelated.

This criticism stems, however, from a miscomprehension of the
author's purpose. Čapek planned the work as a satire on all forms
of absolutism. He attacks the absolutism of science, which invents
the Carburator, along with the absolutism of big business, which
insists on marketing it. He attacks the absolutism of modern diplo-
macy, the absolutism of the totalitarian state, the absolutism of

man's sectarian faiths. War is viewed as the use of absolutist methods in politics.

Man, infected by a religious urge, abandons the profit motive at the same time as the Absolute undertakes to create a surplus of goods. In this way the two seemingly disparate themes are united, for these are the two classic prerequisites for utopia: self-sacrificing idealism and unlimited production. For Čapek utopia itself is a form of absolutism; men with varying beliefs could hardly agree on a formula for finding a utopian system. Utopia would require a totalitarian order for its support—yet another form of absolutism.

Nor is it fair to criticize Čapek's novel for its serialized character, as some critics have done. The *roman feuilleton* is in fact an ideal form for science fiction. As Mukařovský has pointed out, the style and composition of the novel are quite consistent in their journalistic character. The compositional principle is that of journalism; there is no hero, and characters enter or leave the novel in so far as they are "newsworthy."[6]

What is to blame is not the form itself, but Čapek's inability to bring the story to a head in a sufficiently imaginative manner. On the philosophical plane, the chief weakness is a naive faith in the innate goodness of "relativistic" man. This results in the sentimental bathos of the final scene, with its beer and sausages.

The best quality in the novel, besides the high comedy of the opening installments, is the reality and humanity of the popular characters, with their colorful vernacular speech. Their solid "folkishness" makes a vivid contrast to the pretenses of human "absolutism." But it also imparts an irritating and bathetic note to Čapek's relativist philosophy.

In 1924 Čapek published a second novel, *Krakatit*.[7] Both in length and conception this was to be his most ambitious effort until the 1930s. Olga Scheinpflugová recalls that Čapek began to work on *Krakatit* to distract himself from the pain of his spinal disease, so acute at this time that he could scarcely bear to sit, stand, or lie.[8] In fact the novel has an intense, almost feverish quality which suggests illness.

Artistically, *Krakatit* is a failure. Perhaps, as in *The Outlaw* or

R.U.R., the mixture of realist and symbolist styles is at fault. In retrospect, we may conclude that the novel's hectic melodramatic quality was not congenial to Čapek's real talents.

But *Krakatit* is in many ways an interesting failure. Had Čapek's intention succeeded, it would have been the most complex and searching of all his writings. *Krakatit* is a sufficient answer to those critics who have charged that Čapek was a superficial optimist, with a banal view of life. In *Krakatit* he shows keen awareness of the problem of evil and the contradictions of the human soul.

The title of the novel is the name of a powerful explosive substance which is the book's symbolic subject. The word Krakatit Čapek derived from the name of the volcano Krakatoa. There is a suggestion that the unprecedented explosive force of Krakatit is generated by the splitting of the atom—another brilliant anticipation of modern atomic science. Shortly after the completion of *Krakatit,* while Čapek was in England, he expressed a desire to meet Lord Rutherford, who had already made experiments directed toward splitting the atom. Čapek did not succeed in meeting Rutherford, but he was able to have an interview with Patrick Blackett, Rutherford's co-worker, later a Nobel Prize winner.[9]

The plot of the novel is involved, and its events have symbolic as well as realistic significance. The inventor of Krakatit, Prokop, is a young engineer with a strong thirst for life and power. These traits are in conflict with his innate sense of justice. He seeks power to destroy, and creates new explosives to serve his destructive purpose, though he tells himself that his interest is purely scientific.

Exhausted by overwork, Prokop roams the streets in delirium. He meets Tomeš, a former student acquaintance. Seeing that he is ill, Tomeš takes Prokop home and puts him to bed. Falling asleep, Prokop babbles part of the secret of the manufacture of Krakatit. The next day, when he awakes, Tomeš is gone. A young lady, veiled, comes to visit Tomeš, and Prokop falls deeply in love with her.

In search of Tomeš, Prokop goes to his father's house in the country. But his fever has grown worse, and on arrival he loses consciousness. Tomeš's father, a doctor, and his sister Anči nurse him back to health. Prokop spends his convalescence with them, and the tender, trusting, but chaste Anči falls in love with him. But the idyll of the country is suddenly broken off forever, when Prokop discovers an advertisement in the newspaper, requesting him to communicate with a certain Carson.

Carson proves to be an agent for a foreign government seeking to acquire Prokop's intention for military purposes. He invites Prokop to come to the castle at Balttin and work. Prokop accepts the invitation partly in order to find Tomeš, and through him the mysterious veiled beauty.

Once at Balttin, Prokop refuses to sell Krakatit, and Carson makes him prisoner in the castle. There Prokop meets the beautiful Princess Wille, renowned for her coldness and stubborn pride. The princess snubs him, but Prokop conquers her with insane courage, and an even stronger will. They fall in love, but Wille's family attempts to separate them. Prokop, still a prisoner in the castle, arms himself with high explosives and in turn lays siege to the castle himself. This partly humorous reversal of the siege recalls *The Outlaw*. The sense is the same: liberal youth opposes age and tradition with their own weapons. Prokop is overpowered, but wins a compromise: he can marry Wille if he will give up the secret of Krakatit. He realizes the horror this would bring upon the world, but is tempted, and agrees. The princess senses the sacrifice, however, which this decision has cost him, and it is she who gives him up, to save him from his own passion. She frees him from his prison by escorting him out of the castle herself.

Next Prokop meets a foreign diplomat, D'Hémon (or Daimon), who has been visiting the castle. The latter takes him up to a "mount of temptation" and offers him world dominion if he will turn his destructive secret against men. Daimon is the leader of a ring of anarchists which he volunteers to place at Prokop's service. He owns a mysterious radio station which emits waves of a special frequency. These have the power to explode Krakatit anywhere in the world. Thus Tomeš or anyone else who may discover Krakatit will be destroyed instantly after the synthesis of the explosive.

Daimon is accompanied by a beautiful, corrupt girl who attempts to seduce Prokop. He refuses her advances, but treats her kindly. He wonders if she may not be the veiled beauty he is seeking. Finally deciding that she is not, he leaves Daimon, and heads toward Grottup, where Tomeš has been working for another great power in a search for Krakatit. When he reaches Tomeš's laboratory, he is told that Tomeš can see no one, that the invention is almost ready. Frantically Prokop tries to warn Tomeš of the danger; only at the last minute does he flee. The whole town goes up in a terrific explosion just as Prokop escapes.

Prokop continues running along the road, and comes upon an old fortune teller and his wagon. The old man offers to tell Prokop's fortune. Prokop asks why he has encountered so many things in life, but could not find the veiled beauty he sought. "That was your pride," the old man tells him. Prokop tries to shift the blame to his invention. "If it had not been in you," the old man explains, "it would not have been in your invention. Man does everything of his own accord." He asks Prokop to recall how the explosive is made. Prokop suddenly realizes that he has forgotten the secret.

The old man then offers to show Prokop a picture of his beloved. In succession he extracts from a box pictures of the lewd girl, Anči, and the princess. Prokop attempts to look through the box himself for the right picture, but the old man stops him. "That is forbidden... All people are in there."

The old man brews tea for Prokop, and gives him a cup which bears the name Ludmila. He tells Prokop that is the mysterious beauty's name. Prokop asks if he will ever find her. Instead of replying, the old man tells him to drink his tea.

"It's bitter,... too bitter, isn't it? Wouldn't you like a lump of sugar?" Prokop shook his head; it tasted as bitter in his mouth as tears, but through his breast there spread a beneficient warmth."

"You sought to tear yourself apart, but you remain whole, and you will neither save the world nor break it asunder. Much of you will remain hidden like a fire in a stove, but that is well; it is sacrificed. You sought to do things too great, and now you will do little things. It is well so."

Prokop knelt before the fire and did not dare raise his eyes; he knew now that it was God the Father speaking to him.

"It is well so," he whispered.

The old man suggests that Prokop harness the energy in Krakatit, that he use it to develop a cheap source of power, a way to aid man in his work.

Prokop is the creative person. His very name implies this (*proko-pati*, "to tunnel through"). Within him, however, is the ambivalence of creation that may also destroy. From pride, as the old man tells him, his creative powers have been perverted to evil.

The woman he seeks is happiness, or the truth of life. His destructive genius seeks to force the cosmos to reveal this truth, on pain of destruction. The three women he meets are temptations which assail the creative individual. Anči (her name suggests *anděl*, "angel") is tranquil content. The idyllic life she represents has a powerful appeal for Čapek himself, but both he and his hero transcend it. Princess Wille is self-will. She symbolizes the power implicit in Prokop's destructive will. Daimon (the devil) and the wanton girl represent different forms of power, power over the world or over a single being; they also imply the moral corruption which such power brings. Prokop resists all these temptations, except that of pride. Yet all three have something positive which he also rejects: Anči is chaste and devoted; the princess submits her will to his; the corrupted girl is touched by his kindness.

The name of the unknown beauty whom Prokop will never find is Ludmila, a name which connotes love of mankind, and was often used in this sense in puns by the Czech Baroque poets. Prokop's search will never succeed, for he is not capable of such love. Still he can find a part of her by renouncing pride and devoting himself to mankind.

Such an interpretation, though tentative, at least suggests the breadth of the author's intention. The main symbol of the book, Krakatit, is magnificently appropriate as a reflection of the dark power of human destructiveness. The ending is less convincing, perhaps arbitrary, and the introduction of the devil and God seems naive. Čapek wrote, perhaps apologetically, of this to H. G. Wells: "It is a novel about explosive stuffs and dreams and human passions and God; but God is only the end of all—that is His natural place."[10] Still the final scene with the old fortune teller is moving, one of the finest Čapek ever wrote. It is a restful culmination to the breathless intensity of the body of the novel.

A number of influences can be detected in the novel. One is reminded of the London *Times*'s characterization of *Factory for the Absolute:* "a Wellsian idea treated in a Chestertonian manner."[11]

Though the melodramatic style of *Krakatit* is not very typical of Chesterton, the novel does show several points in common with Chesterton's *The Man Who Was Thursday*. Both novels depict anarchists assailing the divine order. In both the reconciliation is in God—and both close with the appearance of a God figure. In both God's appearance gives peace, but denies knowledge; God's peace comes at the price of knowledge.

The use of melodrama to symbolize spiritual drama suggests Dostoevski, of course, and once or twice in the novel, as in the scene between Prokop and the wanton girl, there is a hint of Dostoevski's manner. A more specific influence was that of Jakub Arbes (1840–1914), a Czech novelist who used melodramatic plots and fantastic scientific inventions as allegorical symbols of man's spirit and the conflicts within.

Significant are the dreams in *Krakatit*. Though Čapek was at times rather contemptuous of Freud's theories,[12] the dreams seem Freudian in their symbolism. In the first, which Prokop dreams while delirious, he sees the unknown girl running through a field in which monstrous, cabbage-like human heads are growing. They paw at her legs and skirts with thin, hairy hands. She screams in horror, and raises her skirts higher and higher. Prokop tries to reach her by cutting the heads off one by one, but there are too many of them. In desperation he kicks at the heads, tramps on them, but is caught by their hands and dragged down.

The second dream comes to Prokop in the country. He dreams of a chemical formula AnCi, and only after agonized thought does it occur to him that it stands for Anči. He sees her, goes to her, and attacks her brutally. She resists, but he overcomes her. He reaches down to her and finds only rags and tatters in his fingers.

As the two dreams illustrate, Prokop's love is infused with sensuality; particularly passionate is the episode with Princess Wille. Passion appears as another manifestation of Prokop's self-will, and here again we are reminded of Dostoevski. For Čapek both passion and self-will are clearly linked with destruction itself. Prokop is studying chemistry (formula for destruction) when he attacks Anči in the dream. Princess Wille drives her car ruthlessly over a body-guard to win freedom for Prokop.

This association of ideas is carried into the structure of the novel. The work has two subjects: one the theme of a quest for love, and a conflict between sacred and profane love; the other the utopian theme of the power of human invention for evil. The two subjects progress independently throughout the novel, to be reconciled only in the ending: Prokop's profane desire and his destructiveness have the same root in his pride.

Like the searchers of *Wayside Crosses*, Prokop wants an absolute truth behind the relative, pragmatic truths of his laboratory. He declares: "I know... only facts; *I make them;* they are *my* facts, do you understand? And yet... I... I feel behind them some sort of truth... which would whirl everything around... until it would explode. But that great truth... is behind facts and not behind words. And that is why man must get behind the facts!" (Italics and ellipses are Čapek's.)

Prokop is searching for a part of the Absolute: the law of destruction. But man is incapable of knowing the whole Absolute, and any part which he can discover he can only misuse or pervert. The old man rebukes him for this: "He who thinks of the highest has turned his back on men. For that you will serve them."

In *Krakatit* Čapek sought to achieve modern expression by a complex blend of techniques and styles. The novel mixes realism, lyricism, symbolism. It has elements taken from the genres of melodrama, science fiction, and the detective story. It uses dreams, states of delirium, the grotesque, and the fantastic. No doubt Čapek realized that he had attempted too much, and had failed to unite all these disparate elements into a smooth and consistent whole. For nine years he wrote no more novels.

12. *Utopia Revisited: Two Comedies of the Absolute*

In 1922 Čapek published a new play, *The Makropulos Secret*.[1] It had its première at the Prague Municipal Theater on November 21, 1922, under the author's direction. Later it was set as an opera by Leoš Janáček.

The Makropulos Secret is an attack on yet another dream of utopian absolutism: eternal life. The theme is not original, of course. Tithonus, in Greek mythology, received the gift of eternal life at the wish of his spouse Eos, but the goddess forgot to specify that he be given eternal youth as well. The struldbrugs of *Gulliver's Travels* also live eternally, but grow old as quickly as other men. In these tales, as in the legends of the Flying Dutchman and the Wandering Jew, eternal life is only a curse.

Why then did Čapek take up the subject once again? For one thing, the myths dealt with eternal life after youth had been lost; Čapek varies the theme by granting the possibility of eternal youth, at least in appearance. Moreover, the myths were mere fantasies, while Čapek lived at a time when the rapid advance of medical science made a greater span of years entirely possible.

In 1921 Shaw published his "metabiological pentateuch," *Back to Methuselah*, in which he opined that a radically increased life-span would permit man to develop greater intellectual and spiritual maturity. It at first seemed as if Čapek's play were a deliberate rebuttal to Shaw, and, in spite of the author's quite specific statement that he had not read Shaw's play when he wrote *The Makro-pulos Secret*, critics ever since have regarded his play as an answer to Shaw.

What is likely is that Čapek's play was an answer, not to Shaw, but to H. G. Wells's *Food of the Gods* (1904), in which Wells argues that greater size would benefit man. Čapek, who was influenced very greatly by Wells's science fiction, had almost certainly read *The Food of the Gods*. In *R.U.R.* there is a remark which seems to be a specific counter to Wells's utopian dream. Domin tells Helena that attempts have been made to develop robots larger than men, but that these giants soon fell apart; for some mysterious reason only robots of man's size can survive.

For Čapek titanism is another form of absolutism, and the Wellsian or Shavian superman is a kind of titan. A prolonged life still would not suffice for man to come to absolute truth, but would be sufficiently long for him to become bored with existence. In this Čapek's thought is more modern than either Shaw or Wells; unlike Wells, he is skeptical of dreams nourished by excessive faith in scientific progress. Shavian creative evolution, with its frequent contempt for science, was closer to him, but he could scarcely have agreed with Shaw that conscious will can improve the human race biologically.

In the preface to his play, Čapek writes of its genesis:

This new comedy began to occupy me some three or four years ago, in other words, before *R.U.R.*; at that time, to be sure, I still conceived of it as a novel. Its subject belongs to a group of themes which I would like to put behind me. One more such task remains if I am to get rid of these old stocks of material [presumably a reference to *Krakatit*, published two years after *The Makropulos Secret*]. The impulse for the play was the theory of Professor Mečnikov, I believe, that old age is autointoxication of the organism.

I mention these two circumstances first, because this winter there appeared a new work by Shaw, *Back to Methuselah*, which so far I know only from a résumé, and which also—on a scale apparently much more grandiose—treats the question of longevity. This coincidence in subject is entirely accidental, and, as it would seem from the résumé, purely superficial, for Bernard Shaw comes to quite opposite conclusions. As far as I may judge, Mr. Shaw sees in the possibility of living for several hundred years the ideal condition of humanity, a kind of future paradise. As the reader will discover, in this book longevity is depicted quite differently, as a condition far from ideal and even quite undesirable. It is difficult to say which view is more correct; on both sides, unfortunately, actual experience is lacking. But perhaps one can at least prophesy that Shaw's thesis will be received as a classical case of optimism, while that of this book will appear to be hopeless pessimism.

No matter, my personal life will obviously be neither happier nor sadder if I am called a pessimist or an optimist. But being a pessimist involves, it would seem, a certain public responsibility, something like a quiet rebuke for bad behavior towards the world and people. Hence I declare publicly that I do not feel guilty in this respect, that I have not committed pessimism, and, if I have, then unconsciously and very unwillingly. In my comedy I intended, on the contrary, to tell people something consoling and optimistic. I do not know if it is optimistic to maintain that to live sixty years is bad, while to live three hundred is good; I only think that to declare that a life of sixty years (on the average) is adequate and good enough is not exactly committing the crime of pessimism. Suppose one says that at some time in the future there will be neither illness nor poverty nor dirty toil—this is certainly optimism. But to say that life today, full of illness, poverty and toil, is not completely bad or cursed, and has something of infinite value, this is—what, actually? Pessimism? I think not. Perhaps there are two kinds of optimism: one which turns away from bad things to something better, even dreams; another, which searches among bad things for something at least a little better, if only dreams. The first looks straight off for paradise; there is no finer direction for the human soul. The second searches here and there for at least some crumbs of relative good; perhaps even this effort is not quite without value. If this is not optimism, then find a better word.

The Makropulos Secret has a complex plot involving an old manuscript and a disputed inheritance. The central character, Emilia Marty, is a mysterious beauty whose detailed knowledge of intimate events of the distant past soon suggests to the spectator that she is older than she looks. In the end her true identity is revealed: she is Elena Makropulos, daughter to the Greek physician of Emperor Rudolph II. Her father discovered a formula for rejuvenation, which he tested on her. The emperor proved too fearful to try it, however, and she alone remained in possession of the secret. She has lived over three hundred years, leading five separate lives under different names, always with the initials E. M. Once she gave the formula to a lover, but now she is aging, and needs desperately to recover it. She admits, however, that eternal life has left her without feeling, only with profound ennui and disgust. She fears death, but in the end comes to the realization that eternal life is a greater terror than death. She offers the formula to whoever will take it. Her visitors cannot agree: one, an aristocrat, insists on reserving it as the privilege of an elite: another, a radical, wants to make it available to all. Finally a young girl, Kristina, acts instinctively by taking the document and burning it in the flame of a candle.

The play is not really an argument against longevity, of course. We can hardly imagine that Čapek would oppose medical science's efforts to prolong human life. Longevity for Čapek is rather a symbol of the absolute. Man's life may be weighed against eternal life:

Emilia: Oh, if you only knew how simple life is for you!... You are so close to everything! For you everything has meaning. For you everything has some value, because in those few years you have it you will never get enough of it... O my God, if I could only... once again *(wrings her hands)*. Fools, you are so happy. It is sickening how happy you are! And all because of the stupid accident that you are going to die soon! Everything interests you, as if you were monkeys! You believe in everything, you believe in love, in yourself, in virtue, in progress, in humanity, in I don't know what all. You, Max, believe in pleasure; you Kristina, believe in love and fidelity. You believe in strength. You believe in all sorts of nonsense, Vítek. Each one, each one believes in something! You can live, you... you madmen!

Vítek (agitated): But, excuse me, there really are some kind of... higher values... ideals... duties...

Emilia: There are, but only for you. How can I explain it to you? There may be love, but only in you. As soon as it disappears in you, it does not exist; there is no such thing as love in general... anywhere in the universe... No man can love three hundred years. Nor hope, nor create, nor even watch three hundred years. He cannot hold out. Everything will disgust him. It will disgust him to be good and to be bad... And then you will see that in fact there is nothing. Nothing exists. Neither sin, nor pain, nor earth—nothing. Only that exists which has value. And for you everything has value. O God, I was like you! I was a young girl, I was a lady, I was happy, I—I was a human being!

Emilia's estrangement from life reminds one of that alienation which marks Dostoevski's characters, particularly Svidrigailov or Stavrogin. She too has passed beyond good and evil to that point where everything is infinitely boring. But for Dostoevski there are only absolutes: Stavrogin has chosen one logical escape from the dilemma of God as absolute or man as absolute. For Čapek there is no dilemma: man is only relative. Man's "absolutism" is only a discontented yearning for what he cannot have and what would disgust him if he could possess it. Wisdom, then, is to be content with life as it is.

This does not mean, of course, that Čapek is opposed to progress any more than he is opposed to medicine. Progress itself is a part of life as it is, and progress takes place in the world of relative values. It may be asked, however, whether man's incentive to progress might not disappear with loss of faith in absolutes. But this question can hardly be answered: Čapek would argue that, since real knowledge of absolutes is impossible, faith in an absolute can scarcely inspire man to any real progress.

Hence Čapek cannot accept the Shavian ideal of the superman. For him man's present life suffices for him to be human, and that is the most essential thing he can achieve. Man is more noble as man than as a creature on the way to becoming a god. Even a superman would not be wise enough to comprehend the enigma of life, while, as he is, man is sensitive enough to experience the pain and tragedy of existence, as well as its joys.

Čapek described his play as optimistic, but, as with so much of his work, there are two sides to the coin: a deep faith in life and in the "ordinary man," but a despair of real moral progress or essential change. For Čapek, human progress shares the moral ambivalence of all human action: the same scientific advance which can create new life may in the end destroy us.

Čapek calls his play a comedy; it is not a melodrama, as many critics have considered.[2] Hence it matters little that the audience is aware of Marty's secret long before the personages in the play are initiated. In fact the author's intention seems to be to flatter the spectator by leading him to the solution of the mystery as quickly as possible. Čapek's concern is with character, and Marty is perhaps his most vivid stage figure. A great lady with a contempt for all amenities, beautiful but cold, penetrating but confused, brazen but terrified—her unique personal situation allows Čapek to endow her with a series of paradoxical traits which might seem improbable in any other character. With a great actress in the role, *The Makropulos Secret* is a brilliant play.

In advocating his gospel of relativism, Čapek has overlooked one thing: the tragedy of death. He seeks to persuade us that death is good. But this only can be true as a general law of all humanity; the moment we consider the individual case, we become aware of the profound tragedy of death. Emilia, indeed all the characters of the play fear death, but none of them shows any awareness of its tragic nature. True, such an awareness was opposed to Čapek's real purpose, and would have taken the play outside the realm of comedy. But, by ignoring the tragedy of individual death, Čapek lost an opportunity to achieve a more profound insight into the human situation. Not until (and only in) *An Ordinary Life* did he come to this deeper perception.

In 1927 the Brothers Čapek published their last joint work, the comedy *Adam the Creator*.[3] It was produced at the National Theater in Prague for an unsuccessful run of thirty-five performances. The play's failure may well explain why Karel Čapek wrote no more dramas for ten years, until 1937.

Adam the Creator is another comedy on a utopian theme, and continues the tradition of *R.U.R.* and *The Makropulos Secret*. It shows more influence, however, of an earlier play by Josef Čapek, *The Land of Many Names* (1924), than of Karel's utopian comedies. In *The Land of Many Names* a new continent rises above the surface of the ocean, offering men hope of a new life. But instead of prosperity and freedom, it brings new war, exploitation, and struggle. Finally it disappears in a second earthquake. The similarity of the two plays suggests that Josef Čapek was actually a full-fledged partner in the collaboration, and not a subordinate, as some critics have maintained. Only the optimistic note of the ending—the acceptance of the world as the best of all possible worlds—is more typical of Karel than Josef.

Like *The Land of Many Names*, *Adam the Creator* is expressionistic in technique. Its characters are little more than symbols or abstractions. The events of the play—the destruction of the world by Adam, its recreation according to his personal ideas of reform, his final acceptance of life as it is—all these are subjective attitudes objectivized as reality. Only the ending departs from expressionism, though in its philosophical implications rather than its technique: Adam accepts the world with all its limitations.

Besides the earlier plays of the two brothers, Shaw's *Back to Methuselah* seems to have had marked influence on *Adam the Creator*. Indeed, *Adam the Creator* (and not *The Makropulos Secret*) may be regarded as a specific answer to Shaw's play. Man cannot will to be something better; he only remains what he already is. Adam's repeated comment on how difficult the task of creation is seems a parody of the Shavian concept of creative evolution through the application of will and intelligence. And the superman who is one of Adam's first failures in creation may well be a jibe aimed specifically at Shaw.

The conception of the play is brilliant, and, it seems, completely original. Dissatisfied with God's creation, Adam destroys it with the Cannon of Negation. Adam is characterized as a disgruntled anarchist who hates his fellow men because no one will heed his manifestoes. He fires the Cannon of Negation, an expressionistic symbol of his nihilistic will, and all is destroyed. He alone continues to exist, since he had forgot to deny himself as well. The Voice of God then bids him create the world anew. A heap of earth is to serve as the Clay of Creation.

Adam's first efforts at creation turn out disastrously. Finally he hits on the idea of creating his own double, so that he can discuss with him his plans for creation. He gives life to Alter Ego, who is to think exactly as he does. But he forgets that Alter Ego will treat him as he, Adam, deals with others. Alter Ego turns out quarrelsome, suspicious, and opinionated. He insists on dividing the world into equal shares, and on receiving half the Clay of Creation for himself.

Adam and Alter Ego now undertake to compete in creation. Adam is an individualist, who makes each person different: he turns out poets, artists, and philosophers. Alter Ego follows modern, "scientific" methods, and realizes the concept of the "mass." He makes a mold and shapes his people exactly alike. This dichotomy parodies the ambivalence of the modern radical intellectual, who inclines to individualism, at least for himself, but fancies that totalitarian methods are an easier and quicker way of perfecting the social order.

The first four scenes of the play are imaginative and quite funny. What follows, however, is a rather tedious allegory of world history. The new personages introduced are hardly characterized, and the sense of recognition granted the spectator, that the "new" world is actually his own, is hardly a sufficient reward.

The two camps into which the world is divided engage in a long series of wars. Finally Adam and Alter Ego, deposed by their followers, take refuge in the very hole from which they once dug out the Clay of Creation. They find a bit of clay left, but too little to shape a man with. In disgust Alter Ego kicks the pile. A misshapen dwarf, Zmetek (the word means "monster" or "abortion"), rises from the heap. Disgusted with Zmetek, and trying a new tack, Adam and Alter Ego now propose to appear to their peoples dressed as gods. They arrive to find that their followers refuse to recognize them as creators: how, they are asked, can they pretend to that when it is obvious that creation has turned out so badly? Fresh strife breaks out. Disgusted, Adam and Alter Ego resolve to destroy the world a second time with the Cannon of Negation. They return to the hole to find Zmetek still there, a poor beggar with six children (asked how he got them, he answers that a poor man always has a great many children). Zmetek refuses to allow them to destroy the world, for he intends to stay alive, to see better things. He has turned the Cannon of Negation into a cooking pot, and brandishes it at them.

In the Epilogue we find that a great temple has been constructed on the site of creation. Zmetek, Adam, and Alter Ego are driven off as beggars. Adam and Alter Ego again propose to destroy the world, but the Cannon of Negation is gone. It has been recast as a great bell which now peals forth. It rings as an assertion, though no one can agree what it says. The Voice of God asks Adam if he is now content with creation, and will leave it as it is. Adam answers that he will. "So will I," says God.

The play suffers from a number of inconsistencies. For example, the characters of Adam and Alter Ego change without motivation from scene to scene and even from moment to moment. Nor do the created beings always live up to the specifications for their creation. But these are hardly serious defects in a frankly expressionist work. What is more significant is the play's ideological weakness.

The thesis of the play is vitalistic: life itself is superior to all man's schemes for improving it. But this is demonstrated negatively. The beings Adam creates have faults, but so do those which life creates. Moreover, the play brings no argument on the side of life itself, no example of life worth living. Instead we have only strife, hatred, greed, and stupidity. These are presented as the follies of Adam's creation, but in fact they are life asserting itself *independently of his creation*. The history of the world telescoped in the final scenes is the history of *our world*. If Adam does no better than life, still he does no worse.

To be sure, Zmetek is presented as an example of life creating independently of Adam, and he is intended as the positive figure of the play. Zmetek is a beggar who lives as best he can. He is generous; he has hope for a better future; he believes in life. If the vegetative ideal which he represents does not seem very noble, then we must remember the brothers' distrust in all forms of titanism. Zmetek reminds us a little of Hašek's Good Soldier Schweik in his earthy realism, free of poses and self-deception.[4]

Thus we are left with a double resolution. On one hand life is evil, and cannot be improved. On the other, life with all its ills is good, and Zmetek even has the temerity to hope in a better future.

These conflicting views are unresolved, and no doubt rightly so from the standpoint of the authors. Life is a paradox. But the point of the play remains cloudy at best. To what extent, precisely, ought man to be content with life as is and not strive to improve it? To refrain entirely would be to return man to an animal existence. The question can never, of course, receive a complete answer. But just because of this, it would seem that the brothers might have had more modesty, and refrained from implying even a tentative solution.

13. Tales from Two Pockets

In 1929 Čapek published two volumes of stories, *Tales from One Pocket* and *Tales from the Other Pocket.*[1] Often described as "detective" stories, only a few of them follow the traditional form of detective fiction closely. Some might better be described as "police tales," since they employ professional policemen rather than the amateur investigators so popular in detective fiction. And many of the tales are concerned with aspects of crime other than detection. There are even a few stories in which crime is not the subject; these were presumably included by the author to fill out the two volumes.

Čapek's interest in crime was a by-product of his newspaper work. He himself claimed that the tales were all drawn from life. He added that he deliberately sought to give a favorable picture of the Czechoslovak police and to improve popular attitudes toward the police and their work.[2]

This brought him much abuse from leftist critics in Czechoslovakia. Yet Čapek was aware of the frequent brutality of the police, and if he seems at times to apologize for that brutality, he does so only through the mouths of policemen and within their frame of reference.

In a personal letter Čapek commented on the themes of the *Tales:*

The kernel of *Tales from One Pocket* was the intention to write *noetic* [i.e., epistemological] stories about the various roads that lead to the knowledge of the truth; and so... the detective *genre* forced itself upon me. Here you have discoveries which are pseudo-occult, poetical, matter of routine, purely empirical, and so forth. But involuntarily, in the course of the work another *motif* came up, an ethical one, the problem of *justice*. You will find it in most of the tales of the second half of *One Pocket*... The *Tales from the Other Pocket* are freer in theme; my business there was to look out for flashes of tenderness and humanity in the routine of life, or of a trade, or of ordinary estimates.[3]

The use of the "detective story" as an allegory of man's search for truth is not new in Čapek's work, of course. A number of tales in *Wayside Crosses* are "detective stories," and there are elements of detective fiction in both *The Makropulos Secret* and *Krakatit*. But in these earlier works the mystery which the detective is seeking to penetrate is the secret of the Absolute, and the search ends in failure, even if the "criminal" himself is actually caught (e.g., "The Mountain," *The Makropulos Secret*). In the new tales this quest for absolute truth has been abandoned; relative truth is all that is accessible to man. But man frequently mistakes this relative truth for absolute truth, or at least for relative truth of a wider application than in fact it possesses. It is these confusions of human knowledge which form the central theme of the *Tales from One Pocket*. And it is this modification of the older theme which brings the lighter, more humorous tone which characterizes many of these stories.

Thus, in "The Mystery of Handwriting," a man believes a graphologist's unflattering analysis of his wife's character; the "expert" opinion of the graphologist is of greater weight for him than all the evidence of his years of intimate association with her. In "The Fall of the House of Votický" a historian appeals to a police detective for help in solving a family mystery of the fifteenth century. The detective advances the only hypothesis which will fit all the available facts. But when the historian's treatise is published, the mystery is still described by him as unsolved, for his methods are different from those of the detective, and he cannot accept or use the "truth" which the detective gives him.

In one of the best of the humorous tales, "Professor Rouss's Experiment," a psychologist proves a criminal's guilt by administering a word-association text. But this method fails ludicrously when he interrogates a newspaper man from the audience; the latter replies to each word with a string of journalistic clichés. Marc Vey considers this story to have been influenced by O. Henry's "Calloway's Code," in which a journalist sends coded telegrams to his paper by transmitting the first words of a string of clichés; the paper understands the corresponding second words, which, joined together, constitute the coded message.[4] Vey's finding suggests the possibility that O. Henry's work may have played a larger part in influencing these tales. Indeed, the tone and narrative method of Čapek's tales, with their frequent surprise endings, do recall the American writer. It may be significant that both men were journalists.

Variations on this theme of the limitations of knowledge are found in the tales, "Dr. Mejzlík's Case," "The Blue Chrysanthemums," "A Perfect Alibi," and others. The first story is a burlesque of pragmatist method. Dr. Mejzlík is a police detective who catches a safecracker on the street not far from the scene of the crime. In retrospect he cannot decide what inspired him to stop the man and question him: observation, reasoning, intuition, instinct, or chance. Hence he cannot apply the experience to future work. In "The Blue Chrysanthemums" an idiot girl finds a chrysanthemum of a new color. A search is organized for the valuable plant, but it fails, though the girl herself brings new flowers almost daily. In the end it turns out that the plant grows in a small garden beside the railroad track; the searchers, seeing a "No Trespass" sign, did not venture there, while the idiot could not read the sign. In "A Perfect Alibi" a wife deliberately sends a letter to her lover in an envelope addressed to her husband. The latter assumes that she wrote several letters at the same time and enclosed them in the wrong envelopes, and his earlier suspicions are lulled by the innocuous character of the epistle.

In "The Clairvoyant" a public prosecutor gives a clairvoyant a sample of a criminal's handwriting for analysis. The analyst finds that the writing reveals a character that is cruel and potentially criminal. Later the prosecutor discovers that in fact it was his own writing which was analyzed. Though at first he had accepted the clairvoyant's analysis as genuine, he now takes refuge in the thought that the clairvoyant spoke in generalities which could fit anybody. The story forms a complement to "The Mystery of Handwriting," with the points reversed.

In "The Poet" Čapek presents an amusing contrast between the sensibilities of a poet and a detective. The poet witnesses a hit-and-run accident, but cannot recall the license number of the car involved. But the accident moves him to write a poem, and its imagery, when analyzed, discloses the number: a swan's neck is a 2, two breasts are a 3, and a drum and tambourine a 5. This theme of poetic sensibility and how it differs from other types of human knowledge was later to be exploited more seriously by Čapek in *Meteor*.

It is apparent that the form of the "detective tale" employed by Čapek is quite unconventional. Indeed, there are only two typical examples of the genre: "The Fall of the House of Votický" (and here the "mystery" is centuries old!) and "The Disappearance of the Actor Benda." In the latter story an actor who makes a specialty of living the parts he creates is kidnapped and murdered while masquerading as a vagrant. These are the only two of the *Tales from One Pocket* which give the reader all the facts necessary for the solution. But though they conform to the principle of fair play in detective fiction, by the same token they violate the cardinal rule of suspense: the detective's conclusions are communicated to the reader almost as soon as they are reached.

The other detective tales are truncated: at least one element of the traditional detective story is left out. In "Dr. Mejzlík's Case" it is the logic of detection itself which is missing. In "The Footprints" there is no solution. In "The Coupon" the identity of the murderer is unimportant; only the process by which the police finds him is of interest. In the *Tales from the Other Pocket* this process of fragmentation is carried even further; in some stories we have only the crime itself ("An Ordinary Murder"), or the trial ("The Juror"). In "Telegram" a "detective" deciphers a garbled telegram, but the process (presumably intuition) which he employs is not revealed to the reader. In "Confession" we read of the agonized confession of a tormented man who has committed some terrible crime, but the nature of the crime is never revealed. Some tales ("The Adventures of a Breach-of-Promise Swindler") are mere anecdotes of crime. In the *Tales from the Other Pocket* several anecdotes are sometimes included in a single story.

The reason for this "truncation" is not hard to find. The traditional detective tale is a highly formalized genre, with relatively fixed rules, and an emphasis on the application of deductive reasoning. Its relation to real life, or to the eternal themes of literature, is purely formal. Its world, emotional coloring, motivations, etc., are artificial. Even such simple literary variations as the humorous detective tale, or the detective story with a love affair, are illegitimate hybrids, and have generally been unsuccessful.

The intellectual character of the detective story would seem to have served Čapek's purpose in treating the theme of search for truth; indeed, he says as much in the letter quoted above. But in fact the truth which Čapek wished to stress—the limitation of human knowledge—was a contradiction of the detective story form: the criminal may be caught, but still the whole truth cannot be known.

Another reason for the unsuitability of the traditional form was its stress on deductive reasoning. Čapek preferred intuition and distrusted reason. His detectives often employ intuition to arrive at their solutions ("Mr. Janík's Cases"; "The Disappearance of the Actor Benda"). This use of intuition reminds us of Chesterton's Father Brown stories. There are other similarities: Čapek's emphasis on morality recalls Chesterton. And Father Brown understands the motives of his criminals because he too is a sinner; Čapek's detectives identify themselves with the criminal because they share his motives, at least potentially, as part of their human nature (a theme which was to be developed in the novels *Meteor* and *An Ordinary Life*). In one or two cases we can find more specific influence. As B. R. Bradbrook has pointed out, Čapek's "The Record" recalls Chesterton's "Hammer of God."[5] In Čapek's tale a man sees another man tormenting a boy; he kills the tormentor by making a seemingly impossible cast of a stone across a river. In Chesterton's story the murderer kills his evil brother by dropping a hammer from a belfry; the resulting blow seems to be of superhuman force. In spite of these similarities, however, Čapek's tales are very different in character from Chesterton's, which are closer to the traditional form of detective fiction.

The theme of miracle which had played so important a role in *Wayside Crosses* recurs in these tales. But miracle no longer has such urgency; Čapek is no longer concerned with its metaphysical nature. One story, "The Footprints," is actually plagiarized from "The Footprint" of the earlier collection. A man finds a series of footprints in the fresh snow, without start or finish. Perplexed, he calls a policeman to investigate, but the latter only observes pragmatically that the work of the police is to catch criminals, not to elucidate mysteries (a theme also taken from *Wayside Crosses*, where it is found in the story "The Mountain").

The difference in the two tales are significant. The second story is lighter, more playful; the metaphysical theme of a search for God and the Absolute is left out. The solitary footprint of the earlier tale was a symbol of awe; in the later story there are a number of footprints, and the enigma is humorous rather than awe-inspiring. If the later tale is less weighty, however, it is stronger in execution. It lacks the formlessness of the earlier tale, and there is a vivid colloquial speech. But in the end it is little more than a lighter variation on a once significant theme.

The humorous character of many of these tales deserves comment. The point is not that Čapek has exchanged his earlier seriousness for humor. In the period from 1914 to 1920, stories were his chief, almost his only form of expression. But after 1920 novels and plays took over the main expressive role in his work. The short story thus acquired a secondary function and became lighter in character. When, in the late 1920s, Čapek came to a crisis in his art, he apparently turned to the story as a kind of diversion. At the same time he used his stories as experimental vehicles for introducing new themes, and for perfecting colloquial speech. This experimentation was ultimately to bear fruit in his trilogy.

Several of the *Tales from One Pocket* and a good half of the *Tales from the Other Pocket* are concerned with ethical themes. In his ethics Čapek seems here to be vacillating between relativism and a new absolutism, and the latter foreshadows his later work of the 1930s. One of these tales is "The Record," in which the theme of miracle reappears in a different light; the miracle here is a manifestation of absolute justice. This ethical interest is combined with a relativist viewpoint in several tales. In "Crime in a Hut" a peasant kills his father-in-law because the latter manages his farm stupidly.

The judge, who is of peasant background, recognizes that the murder may be justified in terms of practical peasant sense and love for the land. In "The Last Judgment," God refuses to judge a criminal, for he knows everything about him: the story of his whole life, the conditions in which he grew up. Only man can judge, for his knowledge is relative and limited (a development of the theme of "The Tribunal" in *Painful Tales*).

The *Tales from the Other Pocket* continue in this vein. At the same time they show a heightened concern for style and point of view. Each tale is recounted by a different person, who associates it with the tale told before him. Čapek's purpose in this was not to "motivate" the tales, to make them seem more real by employing an internal narrator, but rather to provide an opportunity for colloquial effect and ethical commentary. The author does not tell us why the narrators have assembled to tell tales, thus evading the obvious question which realism would prompt: is it credible that so many persons would come together simply to exchange experiences? Rather the circle is symbolic; it is the community of men, animated by diverse interests and observing life from different points of view.

The *Tales from the Other Pocket* are the first narratives of Čapek to be told entirely in colloquial speech; up to this point he had generally limited use of a conversational tone to actual dialogue (though in many of his essays Čapek "chats" with his readers in a conversational manner). A new tradition is thus begun in his style which continues in the works which follow: in *Meteor* most of the novel is narrated "orally"; in *Hordubal* and *The First Rescue Party* internal monologue is employed extensively.[6] No doubt Čapek went out of his way to employ everyday speech because he had a flair for creating it; his most colloquial effects are among his strongest. In this way he solved a problem which had dogged him in his earlier fiction; the style of his early stories is too bookish, while the straight narrative of *Krakatit* is adequate but undistinguished.

Several of the *Tales from the Other Pocket* are orthodox detective stories. In "The Stolen Cactus," a collector steals priceless plant specimens from a collection. He is caught only when a false announcement is published that the plants are diseased, and his anxious concern brings him in to inquire concerning the remedy. "Mr.

Hirsch's Disappearance" tells of a murder where the victim is spirited away under the eyes of witnesses, rolled up in an Oriental carpet. The solution here is rather too easy for connoisseurs of detective fiction. Cleverer is "The Stolen Murder," in which the murderers masquerade as policemen, remove the body, and make their escape while the public stands respectfully by.

Some of the *Tales from the Other Pocket* concern humorous or grotesque sides of crime. "A Poetizing Thief" is about a burglar who leaves poems at the scene of his crimes. When his verses are printed in a local newspaper, the thefts increase, so that the paper is forced to stop publishing them. "Mr. Havlena's Case" is about a law student who never completed his education, but makes his living inventing fictitious court cases and selling them to newspapers. One of his "cases" concerns a man sentenced to pay a fine because he had trained his parrot to squawk abusive phrases at an old woman next door. The Ministry of Justice challenges the legality of the sentence. Havlena refuses to admit that he has made a legal error; buying a parrot, he teaches it to insult his neighbor, and bribes her to take the case to court. But in spite of all his eloquence in arguing that the court ought to convict him, he is pronounced innocent.

"The Conductor Kalina's Story" again illustrates the superiority of intuition to rational process. A Czech musician visiting England, unfamiliar with the language, hears two people plotting a murder. From the cadence of their voices he guesses their intention, but he cannot make the police understand him.

A number of stories are serious psychological narratives, and thus continue the line of *Painful Tales*. "The Countess" is the story of a woman who pretends to be a spy in order to be publicly convicted and sentenced. Her sole intention is to impress another spy who does not love her. The story has elements of parody of romantic fiction. "Vertigo" is about a wealthy man who has a morbid fear of high places. A psychoanalyst cures him by tracing his fear back to the death of his wife, whom he had killed by pushing her off a cliff. But the analyst cannot cope with the man's sense of guilt, and when he leaves the patient hurls himself from a staircase to his death.

A tale which stands out from the others in depth and lyrical coloring is "The Ballad of Juraj Čup." A Ruthenian peasant who has murdered his sister tramps for hours through storm and deep snow, to give himself up to the troopers. He admits his guilt freely, but insists that God commanded him to kill his sister because she was possessed by an evil spirit. In Juraj's superhuman journey we have a miracle performed in the name of justice, and in his feat Čapek tries to suggest a sense of the presence of the Absolute.

Čapek's abiding theme of the relativity of truth is given a wry twist in "The Death of Baron Gandara." The baron, a foreign agent and Don Juan, is found murdered. The case is entrusted to an elderly detective whose specialty has been routine murders where the guilty man was either a thief or a member of the family. A younger detective tries to dissuade him from pursuing his customary line of investigation, since the baron has obviously been murdered by another foreign agent or by a jealous woman. But the old man insists on his own course:

"Then they shouldn't have given the case to me... I'm not going to learn new methods. If they've given it to me, then I'll handle it my way, and it will be ordinary robbery with murder. If they'd given you the case, it would have developed into a crime sensation, a love affair, or a political murder. You've got a flair for romance, Mejzlík; you'd have worked up a wonderful case with that material. Too bad you didn't get it."

In the end the old man proves to be right; the murderer is the concierge's nephew, who had broken into the house to steal.

The common subject which runs through *Tales from the Other Pocket* is not relativism, however, but man's essential humanity, often debased, yet still unique and worthy. This new spirit of humanism anticipates the trilogy, and in several stories ("The Man Who Couldn't Sleep"; "The Stamp Collection") we have quite specific foreshadowings of the last novel of the trilogy, *An Ordinary Life*. In "The Stamp Collection" a man's whole life has been distorted by the loss of the collection he so treasured as a child. Suspecting his closest friend of the theft, he loses his faith in others. Only too late does he discover that his father had confiscated the collection under the pretext that it interfered with his studies. He explains the whole change in his life by saying that each man contains within him the potentiality for many lives; experience is that which actualizes this potential.

It is clear that Čapek altered the traditional form of the detective story because he was seeking to humanize it. His use of colloquial style in narration contributes to this effect. He shifts attention from the solution of a puzzle to more human concerns: the problems of crime and of justice, man's reactions to crime, the diversity yet community of human nature. Hence the mysteries which he employs in his tales (when they are not unsolved enigmas) are often banal. The motives of his criminals are the most ordinary: acquisitiveness or jealousy. There is little mystique in crime, and Čapek's criminals are typed by the police according to routine methods. The elaborate tricks which characterize most detective fiction and make possible the seemingly endless elaboration of the form are almost always avoided. Suspense is created only by the narrative construction, by delaying the solution until near the end. Even this elementary rule is sometimes neglected. The interest is concentrated on other aspects of the tale, often quite incidental to the plot.

It is difficult to evaluate Čapek's success in these tales. It can scarcely be said that he created a new genre, though his effort was undoubtedly in that direction. The individual tales range in quality from pedestrian to brilliant, but most of the best stories are those in which he strains least after new forms.

Yet the writing of these stories had great value for Čapek's development. Seen in retrospect, they constitute a preparation for the trilogy, which also employs oral narration and the element of detection, and which is also concerned with the quest for truth. The *Tales* mark the end of a period of relative sterility in Čapek's work and the beginnings of an intense final period of creativity.

14. The Trilogy

In a period of two years, Čapek wrote three novels which, taken together, constitute his masterpiece. These are: *Hordubal* (1933), *Meteor* (1934), and *An Ordinary Life* (1934).[1] For the first time in his work he achieved a firm balance between philosophical and literary expression. René Wellek has described the trilogy as "one of the most successful attempts at a philosophical novel in any language."[2]

Each of the three novels is complete in itself, and may be read separately with full comprehension. Each novel is distinct in subject, characters, setting, even in style and narrative point of view. Only the development of the philosophical themes ties the three works together. Yet this development of ideas is orderly and compelling, and gives the trilogy a close unity.

It seems doubtful whether the plan of the trilogy was clear in Čapek's mind from the beginning. The three novels were published separately; only at the end of the final volume did he add an epilogue uniting them and describing the development of his ideas. This does not mean, however, that the conception of a trilogy was a mere afterthought. The Epilogue makes it clear that at least the final novel was written to shed light on questions raised by the first two. Moreover, the unity of the trilogy can be demonstrated both internally, in terms of development of ideas, and externally, in relation to Čapek's subsequent creation. After the trilogy he dropped the theme of philosophical analysis of human nature; from 1934 to his death in 1938 his works have a variety of subjects, but none continues the major theme of the trilogy. Evidently he considered the trilogy to be a perfected and closed expression of his ideas on the nature of man.

The diversity of characters and subjects in the three novels likewise suggests that the idea of a trilogy developed only in midstream. Each of the novels proceeds from a distinct tradition in Čapek's earlier work. *Hordubal* is a new expression of Čapek's familiar relativism. But here relativism is no longer optimistic; Čapek has finally perceived that his philosophy implies the essential isolation of man and the impossibility of communication. This perception brings a tragic strain, new to his work.

A prototype for *Hordubal* can be found in "The Ballad of Juraj Čup," in *Tales from the Other Pocket*. Both stories are set in the Trans-Carpathian Ukraine. Both heroes manifest a similar duality. On one hand, in the world's eyes, they are crude peasants, idiots, or fools. Juraj Čup murders his sister "at God's command"; Juraj Hordubal returns only love and devotion for his wife's heartless infidelity. But, by the same token, both are "holy fools": Hordubal dies a martyr to his higher moral standard of forgiving love; Čup, with God's aid, makes an impossible journey through a snowstorm to give himself up to the police.

Legend has it that President Masaryk suggested the subject of *Hordubal* to Čapek. This may be so, but Čapek could easily have come upon the idea himself, since the basis for the novel was a news story which appeared in *Lidové noviny* (the paper to which Čapek contributed) on November 14, 1932. A Ruthenian peasant, Juraj Hardubej, returned home after eight years in America to discover that his wife Polana was involved in an affair with the hired man, Vasil Maňák. To conceal her guilt, she had betrothed their eleven-year-old daughter to Maňák. Hardubej broke off the engagement and threw Maňák out. In revenge, the hired man killed Hardubej by driving a basket-weaver's needle through his heart. To make it appear that the murderer was a prowler, he cut out a window with a diamond. Maňák confessed his guilt when the police discovered the murder weapon. He was sentenced to life imprisonment, and Polana for twelve years, though her complicity was never proven.

The use of a news story of crime and detection reminds us of the

Tales from Two Pockets, and in a sense *Hordubal* is a continuation of the same genre. The second and third parts of the novel, which describe the police investigation and the court trial, obviously have their prototypes in the *Tales*. The theme of these last two parts is also typical: the police and court can convict the murderers, but they cannot comprehend Hordubal's pathetic life. Totally misinterpreting the evidence, they conclude that he was either imbecile or deranged. On the other hand, the first part, which occupies over two-thirds of the entire novel, is new and striking. Čapek has rewoven the facts of the news story and changed its whole emotional tone to create a moving portrayal of Hordubal's devotion and self-sacrifice.

In Čapek's story, Hordubal returns home after working eight years in America as a miner. He comes back to discover that his wife, Polana, has sold most of his cattle to buy horses, and has hired a young hand, Štěpán Manya, a swarthy Magyar, to tend them. Hordubal instinctively distrusts Manya, but cannot believe Polana's guilt, even when she will not sleep with him. When the peasants in the tavern speak slightingly of her, he refuses to believe them, and is concerned only for her reputation. To stop the rumors, he discharges Manya. But Polana takes to her room and sulks, and when Manya returns with a pistol, Hordubal accepts the situation, throwing his knife on the ground as a gesture of submission. Here, as elsewhere, Čapek employs symbolic imagery to express Hordubal's psychic castration.[3]

In the end Hordubal realizes Polana's guilt; from a height he observes Polana and Štěpán standing in the yard together:

And he can see his yard like the palm of his hand... Into the yard comes a bright, berry-colored figure and stands and stands. And look, from the stable there comes a second figure, a dark one, it goes up to her and stands there too. And they do not move, as if they were toys. Ants would wave their antennae and run about, while people—are stranger; they stand facing each other and do nothing... it is terrifying how they stand there without moving... O Jesus, if they would only move!

It is significant that Hordubal sees clearly only from the height; the mountain top here serves as a symbol of absolute insight, one which reminds the reader of the earlier story, "The Mountain," in *Wayside Crosses*.

Disturbed by what he has seen, Hordubal conceives a counter-strategy to make Polana and Štěpán appear ridiculous. He will betroth his little daughter Hafie to Manya. This is to shame Polana and bring her to her senses. At first Štěpán consents to the bargain, since the settlement will give him Hordubal's farm. But held up to the ridicule of the villagers ("castrated"), he breaks off the contract. Hordubal then throws him out. Polana again sulks in her room. In a moving scene Hordubal, again on a height, sees the lovers meet (actually to plot his death):

Juraj furrowed his brows to see better. Didn't that look like Polana? Oh no, no, how could Polana be there? At that distance any woman would look like Polana. And from the wood a dark fellow runs out—it can't be Manya, Juraj judges—how could he be coming from that direction? The dark man stops by the woman, stands and talks. How can they have so much to say, Hordubal wonders. It must be some girl and her lover... No, they are not talking. And now there is only one of them, and he staggers somehow. But no, there are two who stagger, as if they were wrestling. And they hold each other so closely that it looks as if there were only one of them reeling. Hordubal's heart stopped.

The imagery here is rich in subtlety: the lovers' embrace is distorted as a grotesque scene; at the same time the reader knows, by indirection, that Hordubal actually realizes what he seeks to deny—that the pair are Polana and Manya.

Seeing the lovers' meeting, Hordubal gives up the impossible struggle for Polana's love. Ill with fever and heartsick he visits the shepherd Míša on the mountain top:

"And what if at the end there is——only an end? Can a man then make an end himself?"

"There's no need," Míša said slowly. "What for? You will die anyway."

"Soon?"

"If you want to know it—soon."

Míša got up and went out of the hut. "Now sleep," he turned in the doorway and disappeared, as if in the clouds.

Later Hordubal leaves, and disappears in the same mysterious way:

Juraj staggered out, into the fog; nothing was visible, only the ringing of the herds was audible, thousands of oxen were grazing in the clouds and their bells were ringing. Juraj walked on and on, and did not even know where; I have to go home, he thought, and therefore he must go on. Only he did not know if he was going up or down; perhaps down, for it seemed as if he was falling; perhaps on up, for it was hard for him to walk and his breathing came heavy. Well, no matter, so long as he gets home. And Juraj Hordubal was submerged in the clouds.

The imagery here, with Hordubal's strange disappearance into the "clouds," has a transcendental sense, as Mukařovský has suggested.[4] The scene is that of Hordubal's spiritual death; like the nameless murderer of "The Mountain," he seeks the absolute of death on the mountain top. He is already near death, in fact, and later the autopsy cannot determine for certain whether Hordubal died from illness or from Manya's needle.

In portraying Hordubal, Čapek has avoided psychological analysis. In its place he transports the reader directly into Hordubal's inner world. Most of the long first part is told as Hordubal's interior monologue. This part is a brilliant example of the technique of "reported speech" *(erlebte Rede)*, of suggesting the personality of a character through turns of phrase which create the illusion that he himself is speaking. In fact, of course, he is not (it is his thoughts which are reported, not speeches), but the author succeeds in catching the cadence of his personality and feeling. The result is an illusion, both of reality and of the portrayal of a whole person. The device is in a sense a trick, but it is employed with complete mastery and control.[5]

Hordubal opens *in medias res* with an example of interior monologue, though it is not clear whose monologue it is: "He's the second from the window, the one in the wrinkled clothes: who would say he's an American? Don't tell me, Americans don't ride on locals; they go by express and that's little enough for them—in America trains are different, and they have much longer cars." Similarly, Chapter II begins with the "reported speech" of an unknown peasant who sees Hordubal returning: "Who can that be coming, down there on the other side of the valley? Look at him, a gentleman in boots, maybe a repairman or someone, carrying a black suitcase and tramping up the hill—if he weren't so far away, I'd put my hands to my mouth and call to him: 'Praised be Jesus Christ, sir, what time is it?'" This unspoken question suggests a reply from

Hordubal, which in fact is never uttered: "Two o'clock, shepherd;
if I weren't so far away, I'd ask you whose cows those are you're
grazing." Indeed, the novel is full of such unspoken "conversations."
With such devices, Čapek introduces the reader directly to the use
of interior monologue; once he has established the technique, he can
make swift transitions in point of view at will, moving freely in and
out of Hordubal's inner world, sometimes simply by the use of one
or two colloquial words.

The technique is carried so far that at times Hordubal does not
speak even when in real life he would; his speech is replaced by
interior monologue. Thus, when he goes to the tavern on his first
night home, an old friend greets him. But instead of the expected
reply, we get a chain of unspoken reflections: "You're a strange
fellow, Husár, why shouldn't you join me—don't think I've come
back a beggar: I've got a fine couple of hundred dollars, even Polana
doesn't know it yet." This priority of interior monologue over
dialogue has its justification. Hordubal is a lonely man, estranged
from the world by the infidelity of his wife and his pathetic love.
The use of interior monologue serves to remind us of his estrangement,
as does much of the novel's imagery.

Besides employing a colloquial tone, Čapek leans heavily on
devices of punctuation: the comma, colon, semicolon, and dash are
used again and again to run sentences together and thus suggest a
stream of thought more fluid than the customary norms of speech
and writing would permit.

Equally complex is the novel's imagery.[6] Its structure grows out
of the opposition between pastoral man and nomad man. Manya is
black, wild, passionate, a breeder of horses; Hordubal is peaceful,
devoted, a man who loves his land and animals. The historical and
cultural implications of this opposition suggest that Hordubal, with
his higher law of devotion and self-sacrifice, is on a more advanced
level of culture than the wild, passionate Manya.

The primary symbols of Manya as nomad and Hordubal as herds-
man and cultivator are mirrored in recurrent images of horses and
cattle. Manya's horses are black and fiery as himself, and their
violence appears as a symbol of sexual passion. Hordubal's cattle
are peaceful and intuitively wise in their comprehension of the

burden and pain of life. The repeated references to cattle, in spite of their intentional naiveté, are handled with skill and delicacy.

In Hordubal's sexual resignation we may well have an idealized reflection of Čapek's own resignation to the continence which medical opinion enforced on him. While *The Makropulos Secret* (1922) and *Krakatit* (1924) are full of eroticism, passion is curiously absent from the tales and sketches of the late 1920s. In *Hordubal* this resignation is pushed to the extreme (though with an awareness of the problem replacing the silence of the *Tales*); passion appears as evil, while freedom from passion is idealized.

The last two parts of the novel, which portray the police investigation and the court trial, are quite different in character. Neither interior monologue nor the stream of imagery of the first part is continued. The critics were disturbed by this break in the narrative, and argued that it destroyed the unity of the novel. The interior monologue ceases, of course, with Hordubal's death, and is replaced by the language of the police and the court, pragmatic or officious. In fact the change in tone and point of view is entirely natural; the break is a deliberate irony which emphasizes the pathos of Hordubal's death. Moreover, it contributes to the philosophical point of the novel: Hordubal's love and his self-sacrificing devotion can never be understood by others. Hence the stream of interior monologue must cease, for the police and court can never enter into Hordubal's world of ideas. But the reader can comprehend Hordubal's nature, and here too is irony, perhaps unintended; through the miracle of art Čapek has achieved that very communication which the novel's thesis denies. Nor does this contradiction impoverish the work; the irony has its meaning as a part of the significance of the trilogy as a whole: each man's loneliness is his own and incommunicable, but all men share the same nature.

The second part of the novel is a study of the characters of the two policemen and the physician who investigate the murder. Each differs according to his profession and experience. The elder policeman, who knows the peasants well, tries to persuade the doctor to attribute Hordubal's death to natural causes, since it is not clear whether he died from inflammation of the lungs or from stabbing. The younger policeman, a recruit burning to distinguish himself, is properly indignant at such a suggestion. The physician does not really care, but feels, from the medical point of view, that murder is the more interesting possibility, since he is not quite certain of the nature of the thin pointed object which pierced Hordubal's heart.

In the trial (the third part of the novel) Čapek emphasizes the contrast between the facts as we already know them, and the constructions, distorted by legal phraseology and argumentation, which the court places upon them. In both these final parts we have a conflict of relativisms, of course, and the ironies which Čapek creates here are essentially like those of the *Tales*. The novel concludes with a symbolic reminder of Hordubal's loneliness. The police have sent Hordubal's heart to a specialist for examination to determine the exact cause of death. Later it disappears. The book closes with a single isolated sentence: "The heart of Juraj Hordubal was lost somewhere and never buried."

In his journal for *The Counterfeiters*, André Gide suggested a new form for the novel: "I would prefer that events never be related directly by the author, but rather laid bare (and several times, from different points of view) by the characters on whom those very events have had some influence. I would prefer that, in the narrative they would tell, these events should appear slightly distorted."[7]

There is no especial reason to suppose that Čapek was familiar with Gide's *Journal* when he wrote *Meteor*, though he may well have known it. The form of *Meteor* grows out of the development of his relativist thought. To approach a single event, or the events of a man's life, from a series of disparate points of view, is an idea implicit in much of his earlier work. It is an idea calculated to broaden the expressive possibilities of the novel, as the quotation from Gide suggests. Normally a character who recounts an event will at the same time *communicate* that event to the reader, and whatever personal coloring his account takes on will be slight, merely enough to bring the recital into harmony with his fictional personality. This limitation is necessary if exposition is to be orderly. But if this expository convention can be thrown over, a whole new world of expressive possibilities is open to the novelist.

It is possible that both Gide and Čapek had a common source for their inspiration in "literary cubism." The cubist painting gives us a series of images, each slightly "distorted" in that each is a different point of view. After *Wayside Crosses* Čapek had neglected this technique for many years; now suddenly he returns to it in *Meteor*.

There may well have been another, purely philosophical, influence on Čapek's conception. Shortly before he wrote *Meteor*, two philosophers, Ortega y Gasset and Karl Mannheim, developed independently a doctrine of "epistemological perspectivism."[8] Both thinkers were seeking to escape from the implications of relativism. If there is no "absolute truth," then everyone is somehow "right," for his point of view will inevitably deviate from another's. Hence truth would not exist, except for each individual. Ortega and Mannheim attempted to break away from this anarchy of individual "truths" (again in a "cubist" spirit) by pointing out the analogy of diverse points of view created by different perspectives. As Ortega expresses it:

Two men may look, from different view-points, at the same landscape. Yet they do not see the same thing... The part which, in the one case, occupies the foreground, and is thrown into high relief in all its details, is, in the other case, the background, and remains obscure and vague in its appearance... It would be... senseless if, when our spectators found that their views of the landscape did not agree, they concluded that both views were illusory. Such a conclusion would involve belief in the existence of a third landscape, an authentic one... An archetypal landscape of this kind does not and cannot exist. Cosmic reality is such that it can only be seen in a single definite perspective. Perspective is one of the component parts of reality.[9]

The logical consequence of perspectivism is the cooperative nature of the search for truth. A true portrait of a table would combine all possible perspectives of a table. In the same way, divergent accounts of an event do not necessarily conflict, but may be integrated to create a truth of a wider frame of reference. This cooperative character of truth is especially stressed by Mannheim. And in *Meteor* Čapek likewise suggests that the varying accounts of his fictional narrators may be at least partly corroborated. Thus, though the technique of divergent accounts of a single event grows out of Čapek's relativism, it suggests a means for transcending relativism.[10]

In *Meteor* three persons try to reconstruct the life of an unknown man. A stranger has been fatally injured in a plane crash, and dies without speaking. He has no identification, but there is a small amount of "objective" evidence, largely medical in nature. He has contracted malaria, so that obviously he was coming from a tropical country. His pockets contain coins of various nationalities, suggesting that he is coming from an area where the colonies of several powers are in close proximity, as in the West Indies. He had chartered a private plane to fly in a terrible storm; clearly he was in a great hurry. He is evidently a European on his way home. None of these deductions is certain, but in the end they are partly corroborated: the stranger in fact came from Cuba.

Three persons in the hospital attempt to solve the mystery of his life and identity. The first, a Sister of Mercy who watches by his bedside, dreams of him on successive nights. In her account he appears as a callow youth who fled home because he lacked the courage to accept real love; he comes back only after he has comprehended the true nature of love.

The second narrator, a patient in the hospital, is clairvoyant, and uses his gift to intuit the stranger's story. In his account the stranger is a chemist who had hit on a series of formulas for new chemical compounds, but lacked the patience to prove them experimentally. When by chance he reads a scholarly article confirming his views, he returns to claim the discovery as his.

The third narrator is a writer. In his version the unknown is a victim of amnesia, who falls in love with a rich Cuban girl, but cannot marry her until he recovers his name and past. Agonized suffering helps him to recall his identity, and he flies home to claim his rightful position.

These are the bare skeletons of the three accounts; though they seem crude, they are actually woven with great skill into finished narratives. Their bareness and artificiality is deliberate; underneath these banal forms Čapek is seeking to comprehend the nature and identity of man. All the tales are symbols of a search for human identity. In the nun's tale it appears as love, an identification with another person. In the second narrative, it is self-achievement. And in the final account, amnesia is introduced as a symbol of man's very need to find himself and determine his identity.

Each tale expresses a different philosophical point of view. That of the nun is ethical. The love interest in her tale is of course a compensation for the lack of love in her own life. But it is not love itself which is significant here, but an ethical conception of love as mutual responsibility between two persons. The nun defines the ethical nature of man's identity when she says, "Only a fragmentary and fortuitous life is swallowed up in death, while a life which is whole and essential is completed by death." Chance is thus excluded; the sense of life is in its own fulfillment and completeness, which no accident can destroy.

The clairvoyant is a metaphysician. Čapek was obviously fascinated by the possibility of clairvoyance, as his earlier tale, "The Mystery of Handwriting" *(Tales from One Pocket)*, suggests. He uses clairvoyance, however, not as an approach to truth in itself, but as a symbol of intuitive knowledge. The clairvoyant can imagine the stranger's past, for he shares his human essence as a man; what has happened to the stranger is that which can happen to a man. Though chance may interfere with the end result, what is significant is that all men undergo the same fate, and are part of the same stream. The clairvoyant compares the possible fates which different men encounter to the diverse forms in which water may appear in what is in fact a uniform cycle:

When we imagine a river, a whole river, not as a crooked line on the map, but as a whole, with all the water which has ever passed between its banks, your image will embrace the spring and the flowing river and the sea, all the seas in the world, the clouds, the snow and vapor, the breath of the dead and the rainbow in the sky—all that, the whole revolution of all the waters in the world, will be that river.

And Čapek comments in the Epilogue to the trilogy: "Whatever we look at is a thing-in-itself and at the same time something of us, something of ours and personal; our knowledge of the world and man is something like our own confession."

The writer, too, is part metaphysician, and feels this community with his subject. But he is more an esthetician who seeks to justify his role of artist as an interpreter of truth. What does it matter that his "truth" is that of fantasy:

I shall try to excuse literature for its love of tragedy and of laughter. For they are the two by-roads which fantasy has invented so that with its methods, its unreal ways, it may create the illusion of reality. Reality itself is neither tragic nor comic; it is too serious and too expansive for either. Sympathy and laughter are only the shocks with which we orchestrate and comment on events outside ourselves. Invoke these shocks by any means whatsoever, and you will invoke the impression that outside yourself something real has been played out; the stronger the shock, the more real it becomes.

And later he characterizes the literary symbol as one "composed of chance and necessity. Necessity and chance, two legs of the tripod on which Pythia sits; the third is mystery."

Each story reflects the personality of its creator. The nun's is a disparate mixture of romance and morality, which she herself cannot resolve. The clairvoyant's is intellectual and abstract. The writer's is imaginative and expansive.

Yet there is a common denominator among the three tales, and not only in the superficial corroboration which comes at the end, for random facts are not Čapek's concern. What rather absorbs him is the problem of human self-identity, of discovery of oneself. The three narrators are preoccupied with the stranger because they feel a community between his nature and theirs; he and they are the same, at least potentially. His mystery is their own.

The final novel of the trilogy, *An Ordinary Life*, pursues this theme. A retired official feels a compulsion to write the story of his life, just because it seems a trivial and "ordinary" life. At first the account proceeds smoothly enough, as he idealizes his past history in retrospect. He is struck by the recurrence of the same patterns in his life, giving the whole a sense of continuity and identity. A childhood memory of the fascination of trains influenced his decision to become a railway-station official. The lonely child playing by himself with the shavings in his father's carpenter shop grows up into the lonely man who withdraws from his wife to create his own world in the perfect order of his model station. He comments: "The course of life is moved for the most part by two forces: habit and chance." In the end habit seems the stronger; chance upsets the picture and alters the forms of life, but only so that habit may reassert itself more strongly.

Only a few isolated memories disturb the harmony of his concept: a childhood erotic incident with a dark and unwashed little foreign girl; or a wild period at university, when he neglected his studies to write verses and carouse. He tries to suppress these memories; they were apparently only interruptions, after which the patterns wove themselves more strongly. But they return again to disturb him. The further he goes on with analysis, the more complex his "ordinary life" becomes. The "ordinary man" he thought himself to be is only one aspect of himself, he discovers. In succession a whole series of other persons unfold within him, some developed, others only potential: an ambitious but ruthless man, a hypochondriac, a poet and dreamer, a hero who worked for the Czech resistance in World War I, a beggar who loves grime and poverty, a perverted sensualist. All these live within him; through them he can comprehend the manifold nature of human life. He is a microcosm which mirrors society. "Have you ever seen anyone, brother, who couldn't be *your brother?*" one of the inner group asks the "ordinary man." "This is just the reason why we can know and understand plurality, because we ourselves are such a plurality," the author comments in the Epilogue.

This paradox of simple and complex, unity and plurality, unfolds into a second paradox, the opposition of the ordinary and extra-ordinary.[11] "Ordinary life" is itself something extraordinary, something beyond price. This paradox is symbolized in the railway itself, at once the prosaic, dirty reality of technology, and a romantic road leading to the end of the world. In its endlessness it is an absolute, and hence Čapek invokes it in the final passage of the narrative, when the official is near death:

Suppose it's night, a night with red and green lights, and in the station the last train is standing, no international express, but an ordinary local, the kind of "milk train" that stops at every station; why couldn't an ordinary train like that go on into infinity?... Wait, it's full of people, Mr. Martinek is sitting in there, the drunken captain is sleeping in the corner like a log of wood, the dark little girl presses her nose to the window and sticks out her tongue, and from his box on the caboose the brakeman is waving his flag. Wait, I am coming with you!

The quest for self-knowledge is itself a search for the Absolute. Hence the end of the quest is death, for death is that point where the relativism of human life merges with the Absolute. The excitement of the final discovery of identity places too great a strain on the official's heart, and the account of his life is terminated by death. There is perhaps a suggestion of immortality in the final passage quoted above, but we cannot be certain; death too is an infinite expanse, an absolute, like the point on the horizon where two rails come together.

The conflict in *Hordubal* is that of subjective and objective points of view; in *Meteor* it is between different objective views. In *An Ordinary Life* the final possibility is considered: a conflict of different subjective views.[12] The tripartite division of a trilogy suggests the triad formula of dialectic: thesis, antithesis, and synthesis. The three novels of the trilogy stand in this relation.

Hordubal is the thesis: all men are separate and distinct, and no man can know the truth of another's life. *Meteor* is the antithesis: all men are related in their common essence, and each man has the potentiality of knowing another through his knowledge of himself. The synthesis is given in *An Ordinary Life:* there is both unity and plurality in human nature, both within the individual and in the society of men without. But it is unity within plurality; the plurality of persons within us makes possible a link with other men. Here Čapek points to the possibility of finding an escape for modern man from the prison of individual alienation.

Is Čapek's philosophy pluralist or monist? He himself speaks only of pluralism in the Epilogue to the final novel. But in fact, as Mukařovský has pointed out, there is almost as much reason to regard his thought as monistic.[13] The formula is not simply that of diversity, but of a unity and harmony within diversity. In Čapek's later writing, particularly *The First Rescue Party* and *The Life and Work of the Composer Foltýn*, this monistic tendency becomes even stronger.

On the philosophical plane, Čapek's trilogy is an attempt to deal with the problem of truth and human identity; on the artistic plane, it represents an effort to transcend the form of the conventional novel and its representation of reality. The conventional, "realistic" novel assumes that reality is single and objective; the novel of introspective experience, on the other hand, suggests that it is relative and subjective. Čapek avoids both extremes, for he is seeking to reconcile subjectivity and objectivity, relativism and absolutism, pluralism and monism. He creates new forms for the novel, neither objective nor introspective, able to reconcile these antitheses in man's perception of reality.

In *Hordubal*, the most conventional of the three novels, unity of point of view is destroyed. The transition from internal monologue to external narrative reflects the opposition of subjective and objective points of view which is the novel's theme. As yet reconciliation is impossible. In *Meteor* objective narrative is reduced to a minimum: we have only a dying man, a wrecked plane, and a mystery. Behind these slight indications lies a reality of unknown aspect and dimensions. But the fantasy of the three narrators is in turn "objectivized." The author destroys to create anew: reality returns as something deeper, not as chain of fortuitous details in the life of a stranger, but as the very essence of life, which the three narrators share with him.

In *An Ordinary Life* conventional narrative form is again destroyed. To be sure, novels have often been cast in the form of diaries or confessions. But in Čapek's novel this choice is not arbitrary; here the form is organically linked to the theme of the quest for self-identity. And, in turn, the form of the personal confession is violated for the sake of deeper insight. The confession breaks off abruptly, as the hero discovers that he is not merely an "ordinary man," but a host of persons. The placid narrative form ceases, and a hectic dialogue begins, as each of the personalities in turn addresses the others, each asserting its right to be counted. This dialogue is clothed in a rough, clipped style of almost primitive immediacy.

Only time can tell whether Čapek's experiments with the form of the novel have been successful. Perhaps he was more iconoclast than innovator. All three of the novels are analytical fragmentations of the novel form, in which the traditional devices of narrative fiction are laid bare. But, whether or not he has achieved integrity of artistic statement, there is no doubt that the forms he has chosen are appropriate for his ideas.

In the trilogy Čapek finally rescued himself from relativism, without losing the sense of freedom and variety which a relativist and pluralist viewpoint can give. Perhaps the most moving quality of his work, however, is the intuitive love and sympathy which he bestows upon his characters. The spirit of the trilogy is at once democratic and deeply tragic. The blind, inarticulate peasant with his pathetic devotion; the stranger who discovers his true self only to perish; the lonely, "ordinary man," whose quest for knowledge brings him to the grave—they are among Čapek's finest creations.

15. The White Plague

The success of the trilogy might well have inspired Čapek to continue the analysis of human nature. If such was his intention, however, the pressure of world events soon interrupted his course, and he now turned his attention to the danger of war and the need to inspire his countrymen to resist German aggression. *The War with the Newts* (1936) was the first product of this new concern with contemporary political and social questions.

This change in direction may be compared to the break in Čapek's development which occurred in 1920, when he wrote *R.U.R.* as a warning of the danger of modern technological utopia. But there is an important distinction. A utopian order, though seemingly made possible by twentieth-century technology, always remains in the domain of fantasy. No matter how many machines man can invent he can never free himself entirely from toil, if only because new machines impose new burdens, and make possible a higher standard of living which involves man in new tasks and responsibilities.

In 1936 the danger was no abstraction but a present reality. True, at first Čapek attempted to portray the world's plight through fantastic allegories (*The War with the Newts; The White Plague*, 1937), which recall his utopian fantasies of the early 1920s. But this was clearly only a temporizing measure, a resort to a form in which he was already well practiced. He soon realized, apparently, that symbolic fantasy was not direct enough to express fully a danger so imminent. Utopian fantasy could always be misinterpreted as mere fantasy, as some of his critics in fact did interpret *The War with the Newts*. In the works which follow Čapek employs more direct forms of expression. In *The First Rescue Party* (1937), he writes a purely realistic novel about heroism and the need for unity in the face of a common danger. His final play, *The Mother* (1938), is hardly realistic, to be sure, but it contains no allegory, ingenious idea or utopia.

Clearly these are works in which Čapek was struggling to find a new direction for his art. The rapid alternation in forms and styles itself suggests this. One cannot deny Čapek's right—perhaps his duty—to deal with the real threat to Czechoslovak independence. But he had too little time to come to grips with the danger, and he worked under circumstances very different from the tranquil state of mind in which he had produced the trilogy. It is little wonder, then, if his last works show a certain diminution of power.

Two new philosophical questions already implicit in the trilogy concerned Čapek in these last works. One was the problem of democratic humanism. That all men are equal, Čapek had never doubted. But he had always been an individualist, at best suspicious of the powers of state and society. Yet, if all men are indeed equal, if all are potentially the same in nature as their fellows, then cannot individuals transcend themselves and form an ideal democratic society? This is the theme of *The First Rescue Party*. The impulse to this conclusion was no abstract philosophical one; the German menace made the union of free men an imperative necessity. Still it was not easy for Čapek to throw over his distrust of the state so easily. In *The White Plague*, for example, he still depicts the masses as the easy victims of demagogues. Nor can we blame him for failure to solve a problem which no one has solved: the ideal responsibility of the individual to the collective, and its responsibility to him.

The second question which occupied Čapek in his final period was that of reassessment of his old philosophy of relativism. Čapek had never been able to reconcile himself to the ethical anarchy which his relativism implied; the relativism which he preaches so fervently in the 1920s is epistemological rather than ethical. In a few stories such as "The Last Judgment" *(Tales from One Pocket)*, he does imply the correctness of the relativist position in ethics as well: we cannot judge an individual's life, for we can never see it whole. But certainly Čapek never doubted society's relativistic right to defend itself, whether against criminals within or aggressors without. He could attack fascism as a self-styled absolutism, and in *The White Plague* the dictator actually declares that he is inspired by a "higher power." Yet the relativist approach alone was risky. Extreme relativism might well dismiss the whole conflict between dictatorship and democracy as a warfare of two rival ideologies, each of which had its share of the truth. Indeed, the London production of *The White Plague* perhaps implied such an interpretation when it gave to a single actor, Oscar Homolka, the roles of both the fascist marshal and the peace-loving Dr. Galén. Čapek sent a telegram of protest to London, showing that he had never intended such an interpretation of the play.

In his final drama, *The Mother*, Čapek at last reached the bedrock of an ethical absolute: it is wrong, to be sure, for a mother to let her sons go off to war to be killed, but it is right for her to send them when the enemy kills other mothers and sons. The individual's claim to freedom and happiness is only relative, but the defense of life itself is an absolute. And in his final novel, *The Life and Work of the Composer Foltýn*, Čapek finally broke with epistemological relativism as well. Though the novel, like *Meteor*, is made up of various accounts of the life and character of a single individual, these all contribute, in *Foltýn*, to a single and quite consistent picture. But Čapek did not have sufficient time remaining to develop an entire new *Weltanschauung*. If *Foltýn* seems to us stronger than the works which precede it, still it is only a torso, kept from completion by Čapek's premature death. This was the tragedy of his final period, that events forced him to reassess his thought when time itself was running out.

When, in the mid-1930s, the Nazi threat to Czechoslovak independence became clear, Čapek remarked to a friend that he had resolved to write a novel about the heroism of war, a novel which would inspire his people to resist. When the work appeared, the subject indeed proved to be heroism, but there was nothing about war.[1] Evidently the gentle Čapek could no more bring himself to write about battles than he could keep a real pistol to defend himself against attackers.

This novel of heroism was *The First Rescue Party* (1937).[2] Its
subject is the united effort of eight men to rescue three miners
trapped by an explosion. *The First Rescue Party* is Čapek's only
purely realistic novel; here, in accordance with the strictures of
realism, one feels the author's personality far less strongly than in
any other of his major works. The subject itself seems at first glance
to be removed from Čapek's world of interests and talents. We miss
in the novel that authentic note of inspiration, a sense of originality
and uniqueness, which can be felt in the trilogy.

This does not mean, however, that *The First Rescue Party* is a
failure. It is well written, perhaps better, from a purely technical
point of view, than *Meteor* or *An Ordinary Life*. It has well-drawn
characters, absorbing action and a real sense of suspense. Nor is
the subject so remote from Čapek's interests as it might seem. He
was born in the mining country of northeastern Bohemia, where the
novel is laid. He took a continual interest in the problem of mine
safety, and wrote articles accusing the government and the public
of indifference and neglect of the miners' welfare.[3] Before writing
The First Rescue Party, he visited the mines and spent long hours
underground observing the work.

In the novel Čapek reversed the formula he had already applied
to human nature in *An Ordinary Life*. There one man proved to
contain many personalities. In *The First Rescue Party* a number of
individuals merge in a single group which has its own spirit and
personality.[4] The two novels, taken together, supply a humanistic
foundation for a democratic philosophy.

Like *Hordubal*, much of the novel is told as internal monologue.
But here the technique lacks the implicit pathos it conveyed in
Hordubal. Perhaps this is because the hero of *The First Rescue Party*
is in fact external to the action, and the reader unconsciously resents
the fact that he does not belong in the novel, that he has been
introduced primarily to serve as narrator. Young Stanislav Půlpán
is a poor boy who has acquired an education, but who is driven by
poverty to work in the mines. Still, he is never cut out for mining,
and in the end a way is found to permit him to finish his schooling.
As a narrator Standa is a great convenience to the author; for him,
as for both author and readers, life in the mine is something new and

strange, and the author is not obliged to employ more than a minimum of technical terms.[5] But few readers will be able to forgive Standa his priggishness or his stuffy romantic daydreams.

In fact, it is the other characters who redeem the novel. The variety of types among the eight members of the party gives the story much of its animation and contrast. The best-drawn character, and certainly the most deeply felt, is Josef Adam, a slow, silent laborer whose whole existence seems a dogged struggle to understand life. His unhappy, questioning face appears marked for death, and in fact he remains below in the mine, crushed by a cave-in. Adam married a beautiful girl, Marie, who accepted him only after she herself had been rejected by the man she loved. Horrified by the brutality of sexual relations, she shuts herself away from her husband at night. Adam respects her feelings, but has no force to cope with the blow life has delivered him. He reminds us of Hordubal, a Hordubal seen through the eyes of others rather than his own. And it is significant that Adam, rejected by Marie, finds his only solace in his garden, just as Hordubal found his in his cows and fields. Like Hordubal—and perhaps like Čapek himself—Adam turns to the soil to transcend his impotence and to renew his contact with the creative stream of life.

In the final two years of his life, Čapek suddenly returned to playwrighting and produced two dramas on war, *The White Plague* (1937) and *The Mother* (1938).[6] Both plays show weaknesses, but the urgency of the theme helped them to succeed. *The Mother* is the better of the two, and Čapek is said to have preferred it to all his other plays.

The relation between *The White Plague* and *The Mother* has sometimes been misunderstood. The first play is widely viewed as a pacifist drama; only in the second play, *The Mother*, in this interpretation, did Čapek abandon pacifism for a militant stand against foreign aggressors. In fact Čapek, though he was highly sympathetic to pacifism, was never a pacifist.[7] During World War I he had been a staunch supporter of the Allies. His novel, *The First Rescue Party*, is a manifest allegory of the danger of war and the need for free men to unite in resistance.

The "white plague" of Čapek's invention is a mortal disease, something like leprosy, which eats away human flesh. It attacks only persons over forty. This is an intentional irony, of course. Men over forty do not fight wars; they control the destinies of states. A physician, Dr. Galén, discovers a cure for the disease. But he refuses to reveal the secret unless his nation and others will undertake to live at peace. The dictator of the land, the Marshal, rejects Galén's offer; his attention is absorbed rather by the task of preparing his people for an aggressive war. But in the end the Marshal himself contracts the disease, and, suffering frightful torments, yields to Galén's "blackmail." On the way to the Marshal's bedside, Galén is killed by a frenzied crowd in the grip of war hysteria. Thus both the secret of the cure and the hope of peace are lost.

Čapek originally conceived the play as a specific reflection of the Nazi threat to Czechoslovak independence. The munitions manufacturer of the play is called Baron Krug, suggesting Krupp. Galén was originally to have borne a Czech name, Dětina, "childish fellow," or "naive person." But constant protests from the German embassy in Prague made it difficult in 1937 to produce an openly anti-Nazi play. In the end Čapek followed his customary practice of internationalizing most of the names.

In its conception *The White Plague* is obviously related to *The War with the Newts*. Both works are allegories of present-day civilization, and both are dominated by a central symbol of destruction. Even in form, *The White Plague* is reminiscent of the earlier novel. As Černý observes, *The White Plague* is not a real drama. It shows some slight influence of film technique, with its many scenes, loosely hung together. But essentially it is little more than a dramatized *roman feuilleton*, each scene of which makes one or another point for the author.[8]

The symbol of the plague is hardly as effective or as appropriate as the robot or the newt had been. Granted, it does express the horror of war, but it also implies that man can combat war as medicine combats disease. The last analogy is little more than a pious hope, for man's political and social science is primitive indeed compared to biology and medicine. It seems doubtful that political science will ever control human nature in the same way that the physical sciences can control the natural order. Čapek's image of plague does indeed symbolize war's horror and irrationality, but it contains the doubtful implication that war, like disease, could be subjected to a kind of "sanitary control."

The drama has other weaknesses. Čapek has not been able to incorporate his chief symbol successfully into an essentially realistic play. Had he made *The White Plague* more consistently expressionistic, the difficulty might have been avoided. But the point of the play becomes ridiculous when projected onto the realistic plane. Galén has no power to enforce his demands upon the nations of the world; he can only obtain promises. Under the "peace" which he would impose on the powers, scheming aggressors would profit even more against their defenseless opponents. Galén can no more enforce peace through his discovery than can any specific peace proposal, such as disarmament or control of atomic weapons.

Nor is the play entirely free from confusion on the moral plane. What Galén is attempting is a kind of blackmail. His ends do not necessarily justify his means. Indeed, his means are strikingly similar to those of the militarists themselves. By witholding his cure, he dooms men to death more surely than do those who send them to the trenches. If Galén is killed at the end of the play, and the secret of his cure lost, then he himself is largely to blame.

Yet the dénouement (Galén's death at the hands of the mob) is essentially right. Here Čapek recognized the deeply irrational nature of the forces which impel man towards war. The ending implies that any simplified scheme for control of war like Galén's would necessarily fail.

Stronger dramatically is Čapek's final play, *The Mother*. Here there is neither a fantastic symbol nor an ingenious idea. Yet the play is not purely realistic; in fact, with the exception of *Adam the Creator*, it is the most consistently expressionist of Čapek's dramas. The universality of the personages is underlined: the Mother is the essence of motherhood, and her whole nature is that of woman and mother. She has no name. The father and sons are named, but they are typical figures. The father was an officer who died with honor carrying out an impossible command; the sons include a doctor who sacrificed his life combating disease, an aviator who is killed while setting a new altitude record, a conservative and a radical who are killed fighting on opposite sides in a civil war, and finally, a young, sensitive boy who dreams of becoming a poet. These are not realistic figures; rather they represent the idealized nature of man. Their ambition, courage, sense of honor, creativity—these traits constitute for the author the essence of what it is to be a man, and these the Mother can never comprehend.

Another device, which governs the composition of the play, is also typically expressionist. All the men, save the youngest son, are killed in succession. After their death their ghosts return to converse with the Mother. In the Preface Čapek remarks that these scenes must be played without the least suggestion of the supernatural. The ghost scenes are dramatically necessary for Čapek's theme; the men must say that they had to die because they were men, while the Mother must argue that life and love have stronger claims than ambition or honor. But there is a deeper motivation for this ghostly comedy. The point is that the play is in fact a drama within the Mother herself; it is her own feelings that are in conflict, which the author has externalized as the ghosts of her husband and her sons. Love compels her to struggle with them for their own lives, but love also compels her to try to comprehend their reasons for preferring death to life. Though she cannot understand their masculine needs, yet she has an intuitive sense of the rightness of their choice. It is her own stories of the father's heroism which inspire her sons to become heroes in their turn.

No doubt the successive appearance of the ghosts is too schematic. When the first son returns as a ghost, the effect is a powerful one, for until this moment the audience has not been aware of his death. But when a second son similarly appears, the scene is comical rather than dramatic, and from this point the play can hold no more surprises.

The conflict, of course, is one of opposed relativisms. The Mother's eternal nature as life-giver prevents her from comprehending man's need to create, to rule, to obey, to die with honor. Here there is tragedy, for her very role in life prevents her from understanding those whom she loves. Yet there remains an absolute truth on which

Mother and sons can finally agree: death may be justified in defense of life itself. Left with the last of her sons, the Mother hides him rather than let him go to war. But when she learns that the invading enemy does not spare women and children, she herself gives him a rifle and bids him go. Thus she heroically transcends her own nature in the name of life. This melodramatic climax was justified by the imminence of war in 1938. We can only speculate sadly on how the conflict might have been resolved in happier times; could the Mother have found a resolution of her pathetic incomprehension in a more peaceful era? Are death and life the only absolutes—is there no absolute in the process of living itself?

Within the play there are other conflicts of relativist points of view. The two twins, Kornel and Petr, are political opponents: Kornel is a conservative, Petr a radical. They discuss the task of setting a room in order. "Put things where they were before," Kornel argues. "Put things where they ought to be," is Petr's reply. "Dát věci tam, kde jim je dobře," is the Mother's counter to both sons: "Put things where they do well," or perhaps "Put things where they are at home." This is wisdom which Čapek learned as a gardener, for plants cannot be placed by man according to any abstract scheme, but only where they themselves are "at home." The Mother alone treats things *as if they were alive*, and in her sensitivity to their needs we feel a hint of the truth of an absolute. It is useless to argue, as contemporary Czech critics do, that with *The Mother* Čapek moved closer to communism, and that for him Petr's view is superior to Kornel's. Both attitudes are firmly rejected by the Mother, who speaks in the name of life and being themselves. Nor is her reply merely a peaceful "neutralism," a refuge in a golden mean of political moderation located somewhere between right and left. Here is no compromise, but outright rejection of both right and left because both are tyrannical, because they compel. The Mother speaks in the name of love for individuals: "Put things where they are at home." Here again we realize how close Čapek was to a kind of anarchism in his political thinking.

The subject of the play was suggested to Čapek by his wife. We may see in it a reflection of the contemporary Spanish Civil War. But Čapek denied that he had Spain alone in mind. The names of the men in the play are international, though some appear in distinctly Czech forms: Richard, Ondřej (Andrew), Jiří (George), Petr, Kornel, Toni. Curiously enough, the play achieved a certain notoriety in the musical world when it was set as a quarter-tone opera by the Czech composer Alois Hába.

16. Opus Posthumous: The Life and Work of the Composer Foltýn

Čapek's final work of fiction was *The Life and Work of the Composer Foltýn* (1939).[1] The author's death interrupted the novel, but the text as we have it seems almost complete. In an epilogue Olga Scheinpflugová gives his plans for the novel's conclusion. The ending as she reports it is corroborated at several points by details in Čapek's narrative itself, and it is obvious from her account that he had almost reached the finish. The polish of the novel's style likewise suggests that it is near completion. There are no apparent breaks in the narrative until the final one; the last sentence, cut off in the middle, is perhaps the last Čapek ever wrote.

Foltýn is a novel of character, composed of the accounts of a number of witnesses concerning a central personage. This technique recalls *Meteor*, and suggests that *Foltýn* might continue in the relativist strain which had produced the earlier novel. And indeed, the separate accounts in *Foltýn* do differ from each other perceptibly, in accord with the personalities of their narrators. As one of the witnesses says, "It seems to me I've told you more about myself than about Mr. Foltýn." Though the accounts all add up to an exposé of Foltýn as a fraud and poseur, still several of the narrators suppose, in spite of all his faults, that he is in fact a genius. Yet relativism of viewpoint is not the final word here. Though the narrators disagree in their evaluations of Foltýn's character, the reader is never misled as to his true worth. Even in the testimony of the deceived witnesses, the reader can discern Foltýn's spiritual bankruptcy through ironic details supplied by the "omniscient" author. Thus the novel suggests that Čapek had moved away from a relativist conception of truth.

Čapek began work on the novel shortly after the Munich Pact of September, 1938. The subject of the new book, the life of a fraudulent artist, was evidently intended as a 'neutral" theme which could lift the author's attention above the tangle of contemporary events. It is at least possible, however, that Čapek intended this novel of artistic dishonesty as a rebuke to his political and literary enemies, whom he regarded as spiritually bankrupt.[2] But the main theme of *Foltýn* is Čapek's own philosophy of art; this theme dominates the novel as his views on truth and personality had dominated the trilogy.

The hero, Bedřich Foltýn, is a shy young man whose most striking feature is a head of unusually long and handsome wavy hair. This detail, along with the uncertain trembling of his chin which agitation produces in him, is repeated again and again in the novel as a leitmotif. From boyhood Foltýn loves to improvize at the piano in secret. He calls his improvizing "composition," but, though he has a remarkable musical memory, he is incapable of anything original. Still he is possessed by ambition, and needs desperately to win recognition. A wealthy marriage allows him to attempt to fulfill his dream of becoming a composer. He patches together an opera, *Judith*, out of bits and pieces purchased from young poets and composers. He tries to justify his plagiarisms by pleading weakness of musical technique; what is important, he insists, is the conception of the opera, which is his, and not details of execution. But even his too eroticized image of the heroine has no originality, as one of his critics observes. Finally the opera is given a chamber performance by Foltýn's enemies as a joke, and the bankruptcy of his talent is laid bare. Foltýn realizes too late the extent of his moral guilt; he goes mad, and is taken away to an asylum where he dies a few days later.

In the middle of the final chapter of the text as we have it, Čapek begins a long disquisition on art (it is this section which is broken off in the middle of a sentence). Here the author opposes Foltýn's view of art as subjective self-expression. For Foltýn art is the expression of passion; he believes that "the artist is possessed by an erotic deity,... and cannot express this frenzy otherwise than through creation, creative agony and ecstasy... All art is exhibitionism. Artistic creation is divine egoism: the need to express oneself, one's inner being, one's whole ego, as completely and on as grand a scale as possible." The novel is a polemic against this romantic view of art as self-expression, for Čapek a monstrous piece of self-presumption. This section forms a digression within the unfinished ninth chapter. The break which the digression makes is disturbing, and not only from the viewpoint of form; a series of logical contradictions runs throughout the novel itself.

The first of these contradictions results from modern man's inability to fix a precise borderline between psychology and ethics. Čapek attempts to portray Foltýn as a fraud and a cheat, a man who commits a moral wrong when he steals from others. But in fact Foltýn is mentally ill, and unable to judge the moral rightness of his actions. His conviction, in the face of all evidence to the contrary, that he is a genius, is purely paranoid. Indeed, his whole personality is an expression of paranoia.[3] His very assurance that he is a genius is a mask devised to conceal his deficiencies from himself and others. He is careful to provide himself in advance with an excuse for failure: he does not pursue a musical education, and hence can pass off his real lack of talent as mere deficiency in formal discipline. Similarly, his very conception of art as erotic passion is paranoid self-deception. It is very easy to imagine oneself as more "passionate" than others, but the truth is that Foltýn is impotent, and the whole argument is designed to conceal this harsh reality from himself and those about him. Instead of convincing the reader that the artist must be honest, Čapek has created a moving portrayal of a tormented personality.

A second contradiction is related to the first, a contradiction which obscures the borderline between esthetics and psychology. Čapek holds that true art cannot be based on self-expression. But in fact Foltýn is no illustration of this view, for *he has no personality of his own to express*. His whole self, like his art, is made up to bits and pieces stolen from others. Čapek never gives the view that art is self-expression a fair hearing. Foltýn is not an artist, not even a bad one, but a poseur utterly without talent.

To be sure, this criticism is based on a literal reading of the novel, one which accepts Foltýn as a realistic figure. If we consider him rather as a symbol, his import is quite different. For Čapek, he is an emphatic illustration of the truth that expression of self leads the artist into a vicious circle, for self, taken apart from society, is sterile. The doctrine of self-expression is pure egoism; the personality which could assert such a theory would be incapable of creating, if only because it would be unable to get outside itself long enough to apprehend the world about it. The most eloquent self-expression is that of the crying infant, as Susanne Langer has pointed out,[4] but it is not art. Foltýn's egoism can create nothing but self-deceptions designed to conceal his own sterility. Seen in this spirit, the figure of Foltýn is richly significant.

To Foltýn's view of art as self-expression, Čapek opposes his own conception of art as creation of objective reality. Art is an imitation of divine creation. It is an ordering, an arranging—the giving of form to formless matter. Čapek compares the artist's task to the creation of the world by God, and quotes liberally from the Book of Genesis. This analogy, formulated by Saintsbury, was taken up by Herder and through him passed on to the nineteenth-century romantics. But Čapek's emphasis on form is classicist and not romantic. He rejects the subjective accretions which romanticism attached to this analogy of divine creativity, such as the metaphor of the poet as God's representative, or of the poet as a "god" himself. For Čapek art is labor, discipline, technique, observation. Humility and personal devotion to art are the primary qualities necessary for the artist, not genius and inspiration. Čapek's definition of art as a human imitation of divine creativity is perhaps more rhetorical than real, although it is true that at this period he was more inclined to belief in God than he had been earlier. In any case, he is not implying that man ought to engage in a presumably blasphemous competition with God; rather he ought to undertake the highest spiritual task of which he is capable. Work is the chief theme Čapek discerns in the creation story in Genesis (thus, at the end of the labor of creation, God *rested*). Finally, the analogy is presumably intended to suggest that the locus of the esthetic is in the work of art itself, and not in the artist. The work of art is a self-justifying creation, made so by the order, the form which the artist imparts to it.

In spite of the lapse of many years, the esthetics of *Foltýn* continue and round out the speculations of Čapek's first period. His emphasis on the giving of order recalls the cubist concepts of his youth; art is a formal construct with its own laws, one largely independent of realistic correspondences. The artist is the bestower of form; it is inner form, not correspondence to external reality, which gives art its meaning.

Besides *Foltýn*, a number of other works by Čapek appeared posthumously. Many of these were short pieces published earlier in periodicals, which now were collected in book form. Most of these collections are non-fictional, but there are two volumes of short pieces of fiction, *A Book of Apocryphal Tales* (1945)[5] and *Fables and Would-Be Tales* (1946).[6] Most of the individual pieces were republished, but a few of the fables appeared for the first time.

Čapek's "apocryphal tales" employ characters and situations drawn from history, the Bible, mythology, or classics of literature. The author reworks these in a search for new insight, for a truth merely implicit in the original story, or one which grows out of it tangentially. The ideology of Čapek's tale may even run counter to the original, as in his "Martha and Mary," in which he defends the practical, hard-working Martha against her sister Mary.

As a genre, "apocryphal tales" were not original with Čapek. Several stories by Anatole France, such as his "Procurateur de Judée," are prototypes for the form. More closely related to Čapek are two volumes of tales, *En marge des vieux livres*, published by Jules Lemaître in 1905 and 1907, and Lemaître's influence on Čapek is undoubted.[7] Another example of the genre is Maurice Baring's *Dead Letters* (1910), but here influence is more questionable; Čapek uses Baring's letter-form in one tale only. All three writers treat the original source freely and with irony; their new insight is often in conflict with the ideology of the original work on which the tale is based. Both Lemaître and Čapek have stories about Thersites and about the biblical Mary and Martha. But Čapek's treatment of

these subjects bears little resemblance to Lemaître's, and his use of
the genre is clearly original. His stories are more serious and more
closely connected with contemporary reality; they are more than
literary curiosities or casual ironies obtained by playing with literary
themes. Thus, in Čapek's "Alexander the Great," the young con-
queror, in a letter to his teacher Aristotle, explains that he has
given up his youthful dreams of valor as too romantic; his conquests,
which extend as far as India, are actually motivated by the pressing
need to protect Macedonia's eastern frontiers. This tale, written in
1937, is a clear indictment of power policy in Europe on the eve of
World War II.

Čapek's tales often have a philosophical point, such as the expression of relativism and pluralism. In "Pilate's Credo" (1920),
truth is seen in the multiplicity of facts, not in any abstract ideal
removed from the world of facts. The anti-Christian implications of
this view were of course clear to Čapek, and his distaste for traditional
Christian doctrine was perhaps the reason for his frequent, sometimes distorted, use of biblical subjects. In one of his essays, itself
an "apocryphal tale" in miniature, relativism is opposed to Christ's
teaching:

If... someone were to knock at my door and I were to open, and it were
Christ on his way through the world, and he said to me, "As you see, I am
going about once again trying to save mankind," then I should weep tears
in my unbelief and my humility, but still I should say (or at least think):
"For God's sake, don't do it, it will only come to naught. Even if it be
the most beautiful, the most wonderful way, still mankind cannot be
saved, perhaps because there is no mankind; there are only so and so
many people. Mankind cannot be saved, but a man can be helped.
Perhaps this is a base ideal, only to help instead of to save; to help some
one person only, in such and such a place and in such and such a miserable
moment of time, instead of saving the whole world for ever and ever."[8]

In the tale entitled "Pseudo-Lot, or on Patriotism" (1923), Čapek
again contradicts biblical teaching for ethical relativism. God
demands that there should be righteous people in Sodom; Čapek's
point is that there are plenty of decent people, but no "righteous"
ones.

There is a good deal of humor in Čapek's tales, much of it that of anachronism. The characters speak a modern colloquial language, sometimes even slang. Details of life and psychology are often modernized. Alexander the Great discusses politics in modern terms. In "Martha and Mary" one of Martha's friends is named Mrs. Tamar Grünfeld. This use of anachronist irony suggests an absolutist note almost unique in Čapek's work: the community of human nature and experience from age to age.

Another humorous device is the burlesque treatment of "epic" subjects in a lower style. In "Thersites" Čapek observes that the Trojan War had its cowards as well as heroes. In "Napoleon" the emperor discusses with his mistress whether his pomp and power is merely a game played by himself and his subjects; only in love, he confesses, can he be quite serious. But here, in fact, he is most ridiculous of all. Such tales seek to debunk the cult of "titanism."

In the last vein is "Don Juan's Confession" (1932), in which the Don is portrayed as a sexual impotent who seduces and kills in order to appear as masculine as possible. We should hardly expect such an interpretation, close to the classical Freudian one, from Čapek, who had little use for Freud's theories. It is possible that Čapek hit on his interpretation independently; such an explanation of the Don's character is entirely in accord with the debunking tendency of his writing.

Fables and Would-Be Tales (1946) is the final volume of Čapek's fiction. The "Would-Be Tales" are short narratives written for the newspapers; as a group they suffer from lack of seriousness and insufficient reworking. Still, one or two of them deserve mention. "Hamlet, Prince of Denmark" (1931) is a kind of "apocryphal tale," a satire on partisan newspaper reporting. A journalist describes the tragedy as if Polonius were the hero and everything else of no consequence.

Several of these tales concern the favorite theme of miracle, here burlesqued. Specialized knowledge inevitably displaces miracle (a theme repeated from the early story, "The Mountain"). Thus, in "Miracle on the Playing Field," a boy helps his home team to victory by praying for miracles. But then an observer explains to him the rules of fair play. The youth continues to pray, but must now add the stipulation that God observe the rules, with the result that all miracles cease. In "The Man Who Could Fly" a man learns to fly by a simple trick of bounding off on one leg. But he loses his new-found ability at once when a professional gymnast begins to teach him proper "form."

Čapek's "Fables" were written between 1925 and 1938. Many of the earlier ones were revised by the author in 1936. All the fables are very brief; most of them consist of a single ironic speech, usually delivered by an animal or inanimate object. These fables are related to the satiric speeches of *From the Insect World*. Many of them illustrate Čapek's relativism:

> *A match:* Look, I am the eternal flame!
> *A rag on a stick:* Revolve in the wind? Of course not, but one must go with the spirit of the times.
> *Last leaf on a twig:* Long live life!
> *A mirror:* I've got it at last. The world is nothing but my idea. Outside me there is nothing.

The fables are also closely related to the *Apocryphal Tales*, and some of them are "apocryphal tales" in miniature:

> *Ananias:* So he sought to save the world? Why not? But he shouldn't have broken with the Pharisees.
> *Attila:* We too have come to save the world.

Like the apocryphal tales, the fables reflect contemporary events. A number of them satirize totalitarianism:

> *Poles in a fence:* Look at those stupid trees. Nothing but branches and disorder!
> *Ant in an ant-hill:* I've got it! What the twentieth century needs is collective spirit.

The fables written after the Munich Pact are full of a bitter but justified indignation:

> This is progress, no doubt: instead of war, aggression, aggression with-out war.
> There are great and small powers. There are also great and small power-lessnesses [a hit at England and France].
> It's not so bad. They haven't sold us out, only given us away.

The style of the fables is colloquial and concise to the point of bareness; many are masterpieces of condensation. Without doubt Čapek's fables are his most original and personal literary form, perhaps even his most expressive.

17. Conclusion

Every writer's work is marked by certain unconscious motifs which often reflect fundamental conflicts deep within his personality. In Čapek's case, at least three such motifs can be discerned, all of them repeated again and again. All three are presumably "unconscious," not in the sense that Čapek himself was unaware of their presence, but that he was unaware of their obsessive character and their inner meaning.

The first of these motifs is that of total destruction. In "The System," "The Luminous Depths," *From the Insect World* (Act III), *R.U.R.*, *Factory for the Absolute*, *Krakatit*, *Adam the Creator*, *The War with the Newts*, *The White Plague*, *The Mother*—in all these we find an image of destruction, sometimes literally of total destruction of the whole human race *(R.U.R., Adam the Creator, The War with the Newts)*. At times there are clear indications that this preoccupation with destruction is more than didactic, and had its own fascination for the writer. In *Krakatit*, for example, Čapek's hero is obsessed with the destructive potentiality of explosive energy itself. Indeed, this fascination with destruction is the novel's most striking quality.

The second recurrent motif is that of siege: the individual is caught in the grip of insurmountable forces which surround and ultimately destroy him. This motif is found in "The Mountain," *The Outlaw*, *R.U.R.*, *Factory for the Absolute* (an episode on a cannibal island), a crime story called "The End of Oplatka," in which a criminal is hunted down by the police, *The War with the Newts* (the human race surrounded by newts), *The White Plague* (Dr. Galén killed by a mob), *The First Rescue Party* (the men trapped in the mine), *The Mother* (the father's death in colonial fighting). In *The Life and Work of the Composer Foltýn*, Foltýn is trapped on the stage at the performance of his opera by the plaudits of his public, who insist that he remain there so that they can relish their joke to the end. And in a metaphorical sense he is "trapped" by the agreement of the evidence against him in the "depositions" of the narrators; their testimony forms a chain which closes about him.

These two motifs are clearly related to one another. The siege is a repressive force, coming from without; explosion is a liberating force from within. Total destruction is the revenge of the individual caught in the repressive toils of society and the world order. Both these motifs show an essential ambiguity consistent with their character as unconscious images. The image of siege expresses anxiety lest the blind force of society (or the cosmic order) should crush the individual. But this anxiety can be dissipated, at least partly, when the author ceases to identify himself with the persecuted individual and makes common cause with society, accepting its repressive powers as just. This cannot be a complete solution, however (since it would involve total self-abnegation), and hence the ambiguity in Čapek's treatment of the motif. Sometimes he identifies himself with the individual within the siege circle, sometimes with society without. In "The Mountain" and "The End of Oplatka" the external force is accepted as just. But in two other instances the individual turns the tables and himself lays siege to the besieging force without. In *The Outlaw* the hero turns the professor's fortress of conventional morality against him, and makes it a stronghold of youthful revolt. And in *Krakatit* Prokop lays siege to the very castle in which he has been kept prisoner by those who seek to obtain the secret of his discovery. This sudden reversal, this unexpected revolt against seemingly impossible force, is clearly a fantasy wish for the decisive triumph of the individual will over the social or cosmic order.

In *R.U.R.* and *The War with the Newts* the image expresses an even more complex meaning. The individual cannot, of course, "lay siege" to society, except (as in *The Outlaw* or *Krakatit*) in a spirit of fantasy or exaggerated comedy. But he can express his hostility toward society by imagining that its own weapons are turned against it, that society itself undergoes assault and siege from without. True, this requires the invention of a second "society" (robots or newts); the trick of imagination itself suggests that the whole conception is rooted in a fantasy wish. At the same time the writer gains moral superiority over the very society he resents, for it is he who has pointed out the danger.

Equally ambiguous is the motif of destruction. If the image of siege is born of anxiety, that of destruction expresses Čapek's hostility toward society; destruction becomes a fancied revenge for the torments of living in siege, as well as a release from that siege. But hostility toward society must be sublimated, or new anxiety would be felt. Hence in Čapek's work it is not the individual who will destroy society, but society which runs the risk of destroying itself. Here again the writer gains a sense of superiority, for it is he who has pointed out the danger.

The ambiguity implicit in these images confirms the essential ambiguity we have already found in Čapek's view of man and society. By inclination an individualist, even an anarchist, he attempted to reconcile himself to society and the cosmic order. Only towards the end of his life, however, was he successful in sublimating the strain of individualist nonconformism. It is in this final period that he was finally able to discard his earlier view of relativist anarchism.

A third subconscious motif in Čapek's work shows the same ambiguity. This is his anxiety concerning the reality of human personality, which expresses itself in the repeated creation of non-human characters (puppets, insects, robots, newts). As writers on the threshold of literature, the Brothers Čapek used the symbol of the puppet to express their distaste for artificiality in life; man should live as naturally as possible. This concern for naturalness persists through Čapek's work. But living "naturally" presupposes a model, in life or nature, and Čapek has none. For him nature is indifferent to man, and opposed to human civilization *(The War with the Newts)*. Living "naturally" for Čapek presumably implies the denial of civilization; in practice this is impossible (for the individual could scarcely survive without civilized order), and outside civilization man would still have no sure model of "natural" life. The dilemma only becomes sharper: does "natural" life mean that the individual should be true to himself, or to society? If the former, he is isolated and exposed to existential anxiety; if the latter, he becomes a mere integer, a puppet. This dilemma is wittily expressed in *Adam the Creator*, where Adam creates individuals who can never agree with one another or act in concert, while Alter Ego creates the "mass" from a prefabricated mold. Only with the final volume of Čapek's trilogy, does a possible compromise between the two positions suggest itself: there may be no dichotomy, and to be true to oneself and to society may be one and the same. Meanwhile the image of the puppet-robot expresses Čapek's fear of social conformism (the individual who casts his lot in with society may lose identity); it also expresses, perhaps, an inner, unconscious anxiety lest all personality be puppet-like.

Even when they are not puppets, Čapek's characters tend to be cold and lifeless. In fact, the form of much of his work seems to be dictated by a secret need to avoid the creation of living characters. František Langer recalls how the brothers conceived their plan for the story "L'Éventail." They determined to write a narrative with but a single character; a puppet was subsequently introduced to make dialogue possible. The brothers' early sketches lack real characters, as do the Italian tales and *The Fatal Game of Love:* in all these the personages are closer to marionettes than to human beings, and the very conception of character is marionette-like. The personages in the philosophical tales of *Wayside Crosses* are no more than mouthpieces for the author's ideas. Only with *Painful Tales* and *The Outlaw* does Čapek come to grips with the problem of character, but in the 1920s he again retreats. His use of expressionist techniques, and of the forms of the *roman feuilleton* and the melodrama (not to mention his predilection for essays, sketches and newspaper columns)—all allow him to dispense with living characters. In his crime stories Čapek develops a technique for conveying the illusion of personality by means of colloquial dialogue and eccentric traits of character; the effect, however, is one of brilliant but essentially external technique, rather than something experienced or felt. In *Hordubal* we suddenly find a vivid and deeply moving character, but *Meteor* represents a new retreat; the hero is an X (another excuse for avoiding the problem), the three narrators are almost pure embodiments of ideas, while the two doctors are "eccentrics." Still it seems likely that Čapek would ultimately have succeeded in his quest for living characters, for his last work shows that he was coming to terms with the problem of the individual and his relation to society. In fact, Foltýn, the last figure he created, is in many ways his most successful. He is, of course, an "eccentric" (the best handled from this viewpoint), but he also has inner reality and pathos.

This weakness in character creation is paradoxical, for all Čapek's work is animated by an intense concern for man. His literary generation, like the French unanimists who influenced it, reacted sharply against the cold, inhuman quality of much of symbolism and decadence. Čapek's writing is in fact a search for man; once the search for God in *Wayside Crosses* fails, it is man who becomes the focus of the author's attention. The trilogy is a deep and searching attempt to define human nature. Nor can one complain that Čapek himself lacked warmth or humanity; his love of the little man, his hatred of titanism, his delight in the variety of life and nature— these qualities illustrate his humanism. Humanism is, in fact, the common denominator of his work. This does not mean that he found faith; in his case humanism rather implies a search for man, a search kept up in spite of an inherent personal pessimism and skepticism. His critics have often charged him with inconsistency—how can a humanist lack faith in man?—but in fact there is no inconsistency and Čapek's attitude is more defensible than that of bigoted faith.

Čapek was a philosophical writer *par excellence*. Perhaps no one of his generation tried so systematically and consciously to express philosophical ideas through literature. Indeed, Čapek's attempt in the trilogy to embody epistemological ideas in literary form is well-nigh unique in fiction. He is also one of the few writers, even of our time, to deal with the problem of modern science and technology. True, it can hardly be said that he was successful in capturing these fields for literature. Science and technology have served writers and painters such as the surrealists as sources of imaginative images and symbols, but they have rarely if ever contributed to the "eternal" themes of literature, perhaps because their content is too intellectualized, and distracts both reader and writer from the universal subject matter of the human spirit. The subject matter of science and technology is normally cognitive, and as such belongs more properly to the domain of science or philosophy than to that of art, which is partly irrational. In this connection one must ask whether Čapek is not one of these writers (such as H. G. Wells or Aldous Huxley) who are not really writers in the strict sense, but who are able to use literary forms, often with great success, for their own purposes. Such writers (and this has been Čapek's case) are frequently popular among intellectuals who have little interest in literature per se. This is not said in derogation, for Čapek's position in literary history is far more secure than it would have been had he confined himself exclusively to more traditional literary themes. One may grant, for example, that his *Outlaw*, which has an "eternal" theme, that of youth versus age, is a better play than *R.U.R.*; this does not mean, however, that it is a more significant one. In essence, Čapek was an innovator who sought to produce new literary forms by cross-breeding literature with philosophy and science. Only, perhaps, in his trilogy was he entirely successful in his attempt, but the effort itself is significant.

Yet here again there is paradox: Čapek's greatness as a writer often depends not on the success of his conscious intention, but on what has slipped in, almost in spite of the author. *In spite of* his experimentalism, his use of scientific or philosophic themes, traditional literary values abound in his works. In spite of his determined effort to come to grips with life, an unconscious terror of life returns again and again in his work. Though he tried not to admit it, Čapek kept stumbling over the tragedy of life. All his work after *Wayside Crosses* is in a sense a defense against the metaphysical horror which he perceived in that book.

Philosophical fiction (or drama) usually ends in paradox; its thesis gives rise to an implicit antithesis. This seems to be due to the nature of creative literature itself, which does not state ideas in philosophical terms but rather symbolizes them. A literary symbol is no assertion; it is a hypothetical possibility which can evoke either assertion or denial. In the novels of Dostoevski this ambiguity of philosophical symbols is unusually apparent. Dostoevski's novels are about man's relation to God, and again and again they return to the question whether God actually exists. To raise this question as Dostoevski does, is to imply that both answers have equivalent weight and reality for the human consciousness.

Paradox of philosophical ideas is an important trait in Čapek's writing. This follows from the conflicts within the author himself, as well as from the intrinsic ambiguities of ideas and symbols. In *R.U.R.* machines bring utopia, but in the end destroy man. In the trilogy man is depicted as a lone individual, but one who shares the essence of other men. Life is found to be pluralistic, yet monistic; it is unity within variety, or variety within unity. In the final volume of the trilogy, a new paradox appears: life is that which is most ordinary (the essence of life is tradition, routine, and pattern—all of which reassert themself the more forcibly after the disturbances brought by accident), but at the same time life is unique and extraordinary.

Čapek's favorite philosophical theme was, of course, relativism. But great literature must impart a sense of wonder and mystery to life, not deprive life of richness of meaning. An absolute beyond man's comprehension is more impressive as literary symbol than the most inspired defense of the reality and goodness of everyday life. It is hardly surprising, then, that among Čapek's worst failures are his apologies for relativism, such as *Factory for the Absolute* or *Adam the Creator*. His finest works, on the other hand, are those in which, whatever his philosophy, a sense of the Absolute is present, whether in the form of death, miracle, or "ordinary" life: *Wayside Crosses*, *The Makropulos Secret*, the trilogy, *The Mother* and *Foltýn*. Somewhere between the two groups lies *R.U.R.*, and it is a curious mixture of weakness and strength. In it Čapek dramatizes a conflict of relativist points of view, yet at the end there emerges an absolute: life.

Only at the beginning of Čapek's career, when he was still searching for a philosophy, and at the very end, was he free from the relativist obsession. It is too much, of course, to say that relativism had a pernicious influence on his work, for it was essential to his unique development. But Čapek himself evidently understood that it was not an entirely suitable philosophy for literary expression. In the Preface to *The Makropulos Secret* he speaks of a "group of subjects" which he "would like to put behind" him. The reference is to the works he wrote in the early 1920s, the highpoint of his relativist period.

Čapek's relativism was reinforced by the suffering of World War I. Seeing the horror which human society could create in the name of absolute ideas and slogans, he took refuge in the comfortable fantasy of the innate goodness of the "natural man."

Where Čapek's work gives us a sense of the Absolute, we feel its greatness. This does not mean that the Absolute itself must necessarily be present, for here we come up against the ambiguity of symbols. What is important for a work of literature is not whether the Absolute exists or does not exist (for, like other religious ideas, this may be simultaneously true and not true); rather it is that a sense of the Absolute be conveyed as symbol. This we find manifested as intensely in *Wayside Crosses*, a collection full of nostalgia for the Absolute, as in the trilogy or *The Mother*, in which the author at last asserts the absolute reality of life and death.

Notes

1. *An Ordinary Life?*

1. Interview in *Living Age*, 319 (Nov. 24, 1923), 384.

2. This and later reminiscences of Karel Čapek's wife, Olga Schein-pflugová, are found in her biographical novel, *Český román* (Prague, 1947).

3. Karel Čapek, "Z našeho kraje," *Obrázky z domova* (Prague, 1954), p. 10.

4. Josef Čapek, *Rozpomínky* (Brno, 1947), pp. 7–8.

5. *Ibid.*, pp. 11–12. Further details are to be found in Helena Kozeluhová, *Čapci očima rodiny* (Hamburg, 1961), I, 15–21 and *passim*.

6. Reported in D. E. Viney, *Josef Čapek*, unpublished doctoral dissertation (Charles University, Prague, 1950), p. 163.

7. Reported in Aimé van Santen, *Over Karel Čapek* (Amsterdam, 1949), p. 20.

8. *Neděle*, 1 (April 23, 1904), 201.

9. I find convincing Miroslav Halík's argument that the earlier story, "The Temptation of Brother Tranquillus," is the sole work of Josef Čapek. See Halík's comments in Bratři Čapkové, *Krakonošova zahrada, Zářivé hlubiny a jiné prózy, Juvenilie* (Prague, 1957), pp. 252–253.

10. See M. Halík, *ibid.;* Josef Čapek in *Rozpravy Aventina*, 2 (Oct. 7, 1926), 3; Ladislav Bulín, "Poznámka o spolupráci mladých Čapků," *Kytice*, 3 (Oct., 1948), 352–58.

11. Edmond Konrád, *Nač vzpomenu* (Prague, 1957), pp. 165–66.

12. J. Čapek, *Rozpravy Aventina*, 2 (Oct. 7, 1926), 3.

13. Letter to Otakar Vočadlo, December 16, 1924; published in B. R. Bradbrook, "Letters to England from Karel Čapek," *Slavonic and East European Review*, XXXIX: 92 (Dec., 1960), 70.

14. This dissertation has not yet been published, though publication has been promised for some years. Arne Novák *(Přehledné dějiny literatury české)* and other authorities incorrectly state that Čapek's dissertation was on pragmatism. It seems that his original work on pragmatism was a seminar paper.

15. *O věcech obecných* (Prague, 1932), p. 148.

16. See "Starý hrabě" and "Starý vlastenec," *Lidové noviny*, July 30, 1925 and March 25, 1934; reprinted in *Ratolest a vavřín* (Prague, 1947), pp. 97–105 and 297–99.

17. Miroslav Rutte, *Tvář pod maskou* (Prague, 1926), pp. 108–10.

18. Reported in R. K. Bednář, *Chief Post-War Czechoslovak Dramatists*, unpublished doctoral dissertation (Charles University, Prague, Feb., 1933), p. 204.

19. *Přítomnost*, 1 (Sept. 11, 1924), 560.

20. Ladislav Tůma-Zevloun, *Alej vzpomínek* (Prague, 1958), pp. 136–37.

21. "Co s literáty," *Sloupkový ambit* (Prague, 1957), pp. 238–40.

22. B. R. Bradbrook, p. 72.

23. "Karel Čapek o sobě," *Rozpravy Aventina*, 1 (Sept., 1925), 1–2.

24. Vilém Závada, "Hovory s Karlem Čapkem," *Rozpravy Aventina*, 7 (Oct., 1931), 41–42.

25. This confession makes an amusing contrast with Čapek's articles of the same period, in which he complains of lack of public interest in the theater. See, for example, "40,000" (1922), *Sloupkový ambit* (Prague, 1957), pp. 215–17.

26. As children the Brothers Čapek are known to have read books of adventure, travel, and fantasy, such as the novels of Jules Verne and Karl May, also popular works on astronomy by Flammarion. See *Josef Čapek o sobě* (Prague, 1958), p. 21.

27. "Karel Čapek o sobě," *Rozpravy Aventina*, 1 (Sept., 1925), 41–42.

28. *New York Post*, Feb. 23, 1925.

29. English translation as *President Masaryk Tells His Story* (1935), and *Masaryk on Thought and Life*, trans. M. and R. Weatherall (1938).

30. E. Konrád, p. 174.

31. See E. Konrád, "Karel Čapek politicky," *Přítomnost*, 16 (Jan. 18, 1939), 42–44.

32. "O tom socialismu," *O věcech obecných*, pp. 132–38.

33. *Pravda*, June 18, 1936, p. 5.

34. "Kraj Jiráskův," *Obrázky z domova* (Prague, 1954), p. 11.

35. E. Konrád, *Nač vzpomenu*, pp. 178–79.

36. "Pozdravy," *Obrázky z domova*, p. 126.
37. *Daily Express*, Dec. 27, 1938.

2. *Back to Someone*

1. These terms are also used in a more restricted sense to designate a group of writers of this younger generation who were actually influenced by pragmatist philosophy: the Brothers Čapek, František Langer, Miroslav Rutte, and the critic Josef Kodíček.

2. "Almanach na rok 1914," *Lidové noviny*, 43:62 (Feb. 4, 1935).

3. See Čapek's comments in "Hledá se generace," *Přítomnost*, 1:11 (March 27, 1924), pp. 165–66. See also his articles on the "Čapek generation" in *O věcech obecných* (Prague, 1932), pp. 138–56.

4. "Almanach na rok 1914," *Lidové noviny*, 43:62 (Feb. 4, 1935).

5. *Umělecký měsíčník*, 1 (1911–1912), 111–12.

6. *Přehled*, 12:15 (Jan. 30, 1914), 271–72.

7. *Ibid.*, 11:18 (Jan. 24, 1913), 301–3.

8. *Ibid.*, 12:21–22 (1914), 379–81, 398–99.

9. See František Götz, "Spor generací," *Host*, 3:6–7 (1923–1924), 152–55.

10. *Přehled*, 12:16–17 (1914), 287–89, 293–94.

11. *Stopa*, 1:19 (1910–1911), 594–96.

12. *Přehled*, 8:44 (July 29, 1910), 781–82.

13. "Úvahy Američana," *Přehled*, 11:51 (Sept. 15, 1913), 837–38.

3. *Spring Improvisations*

1. *Stopa*, 1:5 (1910–1911), p. 147.

2. This last tale has never been reprinted; it is found in *Lidové noviny*, Nov. 14, 1908, p. 9.

4. *Ex Centro; or, The Fateful Game of Love*

1. František Khol had published Czech tales in the neo-classical style as early as 1908.

2. These tales were later republished in the collection *Zářivé hlubiny* (1916), along with the stories discussed in the next chapter.

3. Recently "Ex Centro" has been republished in the collection *Krakonošova zahrada, Zářivé hlubiny, Juvenilie* (Prague, 1957).

4. An early story by the Brothers Čapek, "An Edifying Tale" (1908), treats the death of H. L. J. Droz, the creator of the puppet of "L'Eventail." Droz, a real person, was an eighteenth-century inventor, celebrated for his mechanical puppets. The story depicts him as expressing regret

that he has devoted his whole life to creating a mechanical imitation of life rather than to life itself. The authors were probably unfair to the real Droz, who also invented artificial limbs for amputees. "An Edifying Tale" has been republished only recently, in *Krakonošova zahrada, Zářivé hlubiny, Juvenilie*.

5. *The Luminous Depths*

1. The 1916 edition of *Zářivé hlubiny* also included *Lásky hra osudná*, though the play later appeared separately in 1922, and was therefore omitted from the second edition of *Zářivé hlubiny* (1924).

2. See L. Bulín, "Poznámka o spolupráci mladých Čapků," *Kytice*, 3 (Oct. 1948), 357–58.

3. See *Le Matin*, May 11 to June 12, 1911: "Le mystère de la passerelle," or "La disparition de M. d'Abbadie d'Arrast."

4. Another story in the collection, "The Living Flame," by Josef Čapek, shows a less ambiguously optimistic evaluation of life. A dying sailor, encouraged by a priest to confess his sins, insists that he has nothing to confess, for his whole life was a collection of diverse and marvelous experiences, of value in themselves.

5. There is an English translation of "The Island" in *Selected Czech Tales* (Oxford University Press, 1925).

6. Miroslav Rutte, *Nové evropské umění a básnictví* (Prague, 1923), pp. 154–55.

6. *The Lost Way*

1. One story, "The Footprint," has been translated into English as "The Imprint," in R. Eaton, ed., *Best Continental Short Stories of 1923–24* (New York, 1924).

2. Letter of January 14, 1928, quoted in *Boží muka, Trapné povídky* (Prague, 1958), pp. 213–14.

3. "Mluvím dále," *Lidové noviny*, 31:301 (June 18, 1922), 1–2.

4. "Holmesiana čili o detektivkách," *Marsyas čili na okraj literatury* (Prague, 1931).

5. Jan Mukařovský, *Kapitoly z české poetiky* (Prague, 1948), II, 329–30.

6. See Čapek's article, "Literární poznámky o lidskosti," *Umělecký měsíčník*, 1:4–5 (1912), 102–5, 135–39.

7. Czech has no article, and the word *člověk* here may be translated either as "Man" or "the man." Besides contributing to the impression that the murderer *is* God, the ambiguity here suggests that any man who attempts to define the irrational for himself is outside human society.

8. See Miroslav Rutte, *Mohyly s vavřínem* (Prague, 1939), pp. 197–200.

7. The Offended

1. English translation by F. P. Marchant and others, as *Money and Other Stories* (New York, 1929).

2. František Götz, *Anarchie v nejmladší české poesii* (Prague, 1922), pp. 72–73. See also Bedřich Václavek, *Od umění k tvorbě* (Prague, 1949), p. 38.

3. Jan Mukařovský, *Kapitoly z české poetiky* (Prague, 1948), II, 331–32.

4. "Mluvím dále," *Lidové noviny*, 31:301 (June 18, 1922), 1–2.

8. The Outlaw

1. The only English version of the play is *The Robber*, translated by R. C. Bednar, master's thesis, State University of Iowa, 1931. A copy is available in the New York Public Library.

2. Preface to *Loupežník*.

3. See Bohumil Mathesius, "Fort-Chabrol, Karle Čapku!," *Kritický měsíčník*, 2 (1939), 24–27.

4. Though I do not share the excessively strict moral viewpoint of Pavla Buzková, there is little doubt that she is right in stating that the play contains the material for a tragedy, and this on moral grounds. See her *České drama* (Prague, 1932), pp. 44–46.

5. See Václav Černý, *Karel Čapek* (Prague, 1936), p. 13.

6. See E. Rádl, review of *Pragmatismus* (2d. ed.), *Naše doba* (1925), pp. 505–8; also J. B. Kozák, "O Karlu Čapkovi," *Přítomnost*, 16:22 (January 11, 1939), 33–34.

7. V. Černý, p. 13.

9. From the Insect World

1. A more literal translation of the title would be "From the Life of Insects." The first published English translation appeared only in 1933, though the play was produced in London and New York ten years earlier. The play is variously known in English as *The Insect Comedy*, *The World We Live In*, and *And So Ad Infinitum*.

2. I am indebted to Roman Jakobson, who has called my attention to the similarity of Garšin's tale to the Čapek Brothers' play. By 1920 Garšin's stories had been translated and published in Czech several times. Jakobson's article on this question will appear in *Ricerche slavistiche* (1962).

3. Again the reader must be reminded that Czech has no article, and the word *člověk* means both "Man" and "a man."

4. *New York Herald*, March 9, 1923, p. 10.

5. "Relativní," *Kritika slov* (Prague, 1920), p. 108.

10. *Will Man Survive: Robots and Newts*

1. The text of the play was published earlier, in 1920. The English translation, by Paul Selver, appeared in 1923.

2. Josef Čapek introduced the word "robot" in his story "Opilec" (*Lelio*, 1917).

3. See Čapek's articles, "Muž vědy" and "Edisonův věk," reprinted in *Ratolest a vavřín*, pp. 106–14 and 88–92.

4. See P. Buzková, *České drama* (Prague, 1932), p. 65.

5. See, for example, Čapek's essay "Rozhlas a svět" (The Radio and the World, 1930, republished in *Věci kolem nás*). The novel *Krakatit* ends with God advising the hero to turn the destructive force of nuclear fission into a source of energy useful to man.

6. "Ještě R.U.R.," *Jeviště*, 2:8 (1921).

7. "The Meaning of R.U.R.," *Saturday Review*, 136 (July 21, 1923), 79.

8. Kenneth Burke, *Counter-Statement* (New York, 1931), pp. 49–50.

9. V. Černý, *Karel Čapek* (Prague, 1936), p. 15.

10. Interview in the *New York Post*, Feb. 23, 1925.

11. English translation in 1937 by M. and R. Weatherall.

12. See B. Bradbrook, *Karel Čapek and the Western World* (unpublished master's essay, Oxford, 1958), p. 77.

13. See Václav Černý, "Poslední Čapkovo tvůrčí období a jeho demokratický humanismus," *Kritický měsíčník*, 2 (1939), 50–51.

14. Čapek's satire of communism takes the specific form of an amusing manifesto addressed to the enslaved newts by the Communist Party. This manifesto was omitted without comment from the Czech edition of 1954; it has been restored, however, in the most recent edition of 1958.

11. *A Preview of Atomic Fission: Two Novels of the Absolute*

1. English translation as *The Absolute at Large* (1927).

2. *Times Literary Supplement* (July 5, 1923), p. 456.

3. V. Černý, *Karel Čapek* (Prague, 1936), p. 21.

4. "Nemohu mlčet," *Lidové noviny*, 30 (June 10, 1922), 1–2.

5. See Miroslav Rutte, *Skrytá tvář* (*Vyškova na Moravě*, 1925), p. 145.

6. J. Mukařovský, *Kapitoly z české poetiky* (Prague, 1948), II, 333.

7. English translation by Lawrence Hyde (1925).

8. A. van Santen, *Over Karel Čapek* (Amsterdam, 1949), p. 53.

9. I am indebted to Professor Otakar Vočadlo for this information.

10. Letter to H. G. Wells, June 19, 1925, published in B. R. Bradbrook, "Letters to England from Karel Čapek," *Slavonic and East European Review*, XXXIX:92 (Dec., 1960), p. 65.

11. See p. 101.

12. See, for example, his parody, "Jozef Egyptský, čili o freudovském vykládání snů," *O fantasii aneb k jednomu čtenáři*, (Prague, 1947), pp. 26–35.

12. *Utopia Revisited: Two Comedies of the Absolute*

1. The word *věc*, literally, "thing," refers to the secret formula which Emilia Marty possesses, and not to the legal suit. The play has been translated into English in an adaptation by J. W. Luce (1925).

2. See, for example, J. Brooks Atkinson's review in *The New York Times*, Jan. 22, 1926.

3. English translation by Dora Round (1930).

4. See P. Buzková, *České drama* (Prague, 1932), p. 51.

13. *Tales from Two Pockets*

1. In 1932 a selection of these tales was published in English under the title of *Tales from Two Pockets*, translated by Paul Selver. This selected edition has been reprinted a number of times, but a complete edition in English has never appeared.

2. *Nový večerník*, Nov. 5, 1930, p. 3.

3. Quoted in Oliver Elton, *Essays and Addresses* (New York, 1939), pp. 163–64.

4. Marc Vey, "Une source de Karel Čapek?" *Revue des études slaves*, XXXVI (1959), 59–63.

5. See B. Bradbrook, "The Literary Relationship between G. K. Chesterton and Karel Čapek, *Slavonic and East Enropean Review*, XXXIX: 93 June, 1961), pp. 331-32.

6. See Jiří Haller, "O slohu Karla Čapka," *Přítomnost*, XIV (1937), 747–50, 761–64.

14. *The Trilogy*

1. These novels were translated into English by M. and R. Weatherall; they were published separately in 1934–1936. Later they were reissued in one volume as *Three Novels* (1948).

2. *Columbia Dictionary of Modern European Literature* (New York, 1947), p. 139.

3. See W. E. Harkins, "Imagery in Karel Čapek's *Hordubal*," *PMLA*, LXXV (1960), 616–20.

4. Mukařovský, "Významová výstavba a komposiční osnova epiky Karla Čapka," *Kapitoly z české poetiky* (Prague, 1948), II, 379–80.

5. To date, apparently, no study has been made of the problem of *erlebte Rede* in Czech fiction. It is obviously an artificial construct, setting up a speech level which can move freely and subtly back and forth between the author's point of view and that of his hero.

6. See Harkins, *op. cit.*

7. André Gide, *Journal des Faux-Monnayeurs* (Paris, 1927), entry for November 21, 1920. Quoted by D. D. di Sarra in "Materiali per uno studio sulla tecnica del romanzo novecentesco: Povětroň di K. Čapek," *Ricerche slavistiche*, I (1950), 53.

8. Ortega in *El tema de nuestro tempo* (Madrid, 1923); Mannheim in *Ideologie und Utopie* (Bonn, 1929).

9. Quoted from José Ortega y Gasset, *The Modern Theme* (New York, 1933), pp. 89–90.

10. Miroslav Rutte describes the epistemology of *Meteor* as perspectivism, but does not mention the tie with Ortega or Mannheim. See M. Rutte, *Mohyly s vavřínem* (Prague, 1939), pp. 197–200.

11. See W. E. Harkins, "Karel Čapek and the Ordinary Life," *Books Abroad*, XXXVI: 3 (Summer, 1962).

12. See W. E. Harkins, "Form and Thematic Unity in Karel Čapek's Trilogy," *Slavic and East European Journal*, 15 (1957), 92–100.

13. J. Mukařovský, p. 400.

15. *The White Plague*

1. See E. Konrád, *Nač vzpomenu* (Prague, 1957), pp. 179–180.

2. A more literal rendering of the Czech title would be "The First Work Shift." The English translation is by M. and R. Weatherall, and was published in 1940.

3. See "Pronobis" (1923), *Sloupkový ambit*, pp. 167–69.

4. See J. Mukařovský, *Kapitoly z české poetiky* (Prague, 1948), II, 395–96.

5. See Oldřich Králík, "Čapkova První parta," *Nový život*, 12 (1958), 924–25.

6. *The White Plague* was translated by Paul Selver and Ralph Neale as *Power and Glory* (1938); *The Mother* was translated by Paul Selver (1940).

7. See, for example, his article, "Prosba o milost" (1924), *Sloupkový*

ambit (Prague, 1957), pp. 176–78, in which he argues against pacifism and for preparedness.

8. V. Černý, "Poslední Čapkovo tvůrčí období a jeho demokratický humanismus," *Kritický měsíčník*, 2 (1939), 51.

16. *Opus Posthumous: The Life and Work of the Composer Foltýn*

1. English translation by M. and R. Weatherall, as *The Cheat* (1941).

2. See M. Rutte, *Mohyly s vavřínem* (Prague, 1939), p. 207.

3. Professor John Fizer has pointed out to me that Foltýn's personality is consistently paranoid.

4. Susanne K. Langer, *Problems of Art* (New York, 1957), p. 25.

5. Translated by Dora Round as *Apocryphal Stories* (1949).

6. "Would-Be Tales" is Božena Bradbrook's felicitous translation of the Czech word *podpovídky*.

7. See Karel Růžička, "Na okraj Čapkovy 'Knihy apokryfů,'" *Kritický měsíčník*, 7 (1946), 184–89.

8. "Zklamal nás rozum?" *Přítomnost*, 11:28 (July 1, 1934).

English and Czech Titles

This list is incomplete and contains only titles referred to in the present study. Titles are given alphabetically in the English form used in the text. Titles of published English translations which vary from these are listed with cross-references. An asterisk designates works which were co-authored with Josef Čapek.

Countess, The   Grófinka
Coupon, The   Kupon
Crime in a Hut, A   Zločin v chalupě

Death of Baron Gandara, The   Smrt barona Gandary
Disappearance of the Actor Benda, The   Zmizení herce Bendy
Don Juan's Confession   Zpověď Dona Juana
Dr. Mejzlík's Case   Případ dra Mejzlíka

Edifying Tale, An   Poučná povídka*
Elegy   Elegie
Elegy—The Footprint II   Elegie (Šlépěj II)
End of Oplatka, The   Oplatkův konec

Fables and Would-Be Tales   Bajky a podpovídky
Factory for the Absolute   Továrna na Absolutno
Fall of the House of Votický, The   Pád rodu Votických
Famous Man, A   Znamenitý člověk*
Fatal Supper, A   Smrtelná večeře*
Fateful Game of Love, The   Lásky hra osudná*
First Rescue Party, The   První parta
Footprint, The   Šlépěj
Footprints, The   Šlépěje
From the Insect World   Ze života hmyzu*
From the Life of Insects   *see* From the Insect World

Garden of Kraknonoš, The   Krakonošova zahrada*

Hamlet, Prince of Denmark   Hamlet, princ danský
Help!   Pomoc!

Imprint, The   *see* Footprint, The
Island, The   Ostrov

Juror, The   Porotce

Last Judgment, The   Poslední soud
Life and Work of the Composer Foltýn, The   Život a dílo skladatele
     Foltýna
Lost Way, The   Ztracená cesta
Love Song—Lída II   Milostná píseň (Lída II)
Luminous Depths, The   Zářivé hlubiny*
Lunar Comedy, A   Komedie lunární*

Makropulos Secret, The   Věc Makropulos
Man Who Could Fly, The   Muž, který dovedl lítat

Index